C-109   CAREER EXAMINATION SERIES

This is your
PASSBOOK for...

Boilermaker

Test Preparation Study Guide
Questions & Answers

COPYRIGHT NOTICE

This book is SOLELY intended for, is sold ONLY to, and its use is RESTRICTED to individual, bona fide applicants or candidates who qualify by virtue of having seriously filed applications for appropriate license, certificate, professional and/or promotional advancement, higher school matriculation, scholarship, or other legitimate requirements of education and/or governmental authorities.

This book is NOT intended for use, class instruction, tutoring, training, duplication, copying, reprinting, excerption, or adaptation, etc., by:

1) Other publishers
2) Proprietors and/or Instructors of "Coaching" and/or Preparatory Courses
3) Personnel and/or Training Divisions of commercial, industrial, and governmental organizations
4) Schools, colleges, or universities and/or their departments and staffs, including teachers and other personnel
5) Testing Agencies or Bureaus
6) Study groups which seek by the purchase of a single volume to copy and/or duplicate and/or adapt this material for use by the group as a whole without having purchased individual volumes for each of the members of the group
7) Et al.

Such persons would be in violation of appropriate Federal and State statutes.

PROVISION OF LICENSING AGREEMENTS – Recognized educational, commercial, industrial, and governmental institutions and organizations, and others legitimately engaged in educational pursuits, including training, testing, and measurement activities, may address request for a licensing agreement to the copyright owners, who will determine whether, and under what conditions, including fees and charges, the materials in this book may be used them. In other words, a licensing facility exists for the legitimate use of the material in this book on other than an individual basis. However, it is asseverated and affirmed here that the material in this book CANNOT be used without the receipt of the express permission of such a licensing agreement from the Publishers. Inquiries re licensing should be addressed to the company, attention rights and permissions department.

All rights reserved, including the right of reproduction in whole or in part, in any form or by any means, electronic or mechanical, including photocopying, recording, or by any information storage and retrieval system, without permission in writing from the Publisher.

Copyright © 2024 by
National Learning Corporation

212 Michael Drive, Syosset, NY 11791
(516) 921-8888 • www.passbooks.com
E-mail: info@passbooks.com

PUBLISHED IN THE UNITED STATES OF AMERICA

PASSBOOK® SERIES

THE *PASSBOOK® SERIES* has been created to prepare applicants and candidates for the ultimate academic battlefield – the examination room.

At some time in our lives, each and every one of us may be required to take an examination – for validation, matriculation, admission, qualification, registration, certification, or licensure.

Based on the assumption that every applicant or candidate has met the basic formal educational standards, has taken the required number of courses, and read the necessary texts, the *PASSBOOK® SERIES* furnishes the one special preparation which may assure passing with confidence, instead of failing with insecurity. Examination questions – together with answers – are furnished as the basic vehicle for study so that the mysteries of the examination and its compounding difficulties may be eliminated or diminished by a sure method.

This book is meant to help you pass your examination provided that you qualify and are serious in your objective.

The entire field is reviewed through the huge store of content information which is succinctly presented through a provocative and challenging approach – the question-and-answer method.

A climate of success is established by furnishing the correct answers at the end of each test.

You soon learn to recognize types of questions, forms of questions, and patterns of questioning. You may even begin to anticipate expected outcomes.

You perceive that many questions are repeated or adapted so that you can gain acute insights, which may enable you to score many sure points.

You learn how to confront new questions, or types of questions, and to attack them confidently and work out the correct answers.

You note objectives and emphases, and recognize pitfalls and dangers, so that you may make positive educational adjustments.

Moreover, you are kept fully informed in relation to new concepts, methods, practices, and directions in the field.

You discover that you are actually taking the examination all the time: you are preparing for the examination by "taking" an examination, not by reading extraneous and/or supererogatory textbooks.

In short, this PASSBOOK®, used directedly, should be an important factor in helping you to pass your test.

BOILERMAKER

DUTIES
Under supervision, maintains, repairs and overhauls steam-generating boilers, incinerators and appurtenant equipment; performs related work.

EXAMPLES OF TYPICAL TASKS
Constructs, overhauls and repairs boilers, stacks, tanks, incinerators and appurtenant equipment by performing the following: chipping, caulking, riveting, filing, fitting, grinding, patching, drilling and layout work; burning using an acetylene torch, horizontal, vertical and overhead production welding; and rolling and shaping sheets to required contours. Supervises the work of subordinate personnel and keeps records of work progress.

SCOPE OF THE EXAMINATION
The <u>multiple-choice</u> test measures knowledge, skills and abilities in such areas as: use of tools for boiler repairs, fabrication and layout from diagrams; horizontal, vertical and overhead production welding, burning (acetylene torch) and tack welding; and other related areas.

HOW TO TAKE A TEST

I. YOU MUST PASS AN EXAMINATION

A. *WHAT EVERY CANDIDATE SHOULD KNOW*

Examination applicants often ask us for help in preparing for the written test. What can I study in advance? What kinds of questions will be asked? How will the test be given? How will the papers be graded?

As an applicant for a civil service examination, you may be wondering about some of these things. Our purpose here is to suggest effective methods of advance study and to describe civil service examinations.

Your chances for success on this examination can be increased if you know how to prepare. Those "pre-examination jitters" can be reduced if you know what to expect. You can even experience an adventure in good citizenship if you know why civil service exams are given.

B. *WHY ARE CIVIL SERVICE EXAMINATIONS GIVEN?*

Civil service examinations are important to you in two ways. As a citizen, you want public jobs filled by employees who know how to do their work. As a job seeker, you want a fair chance to compete for that job on an equal footing with other candidates. The best-known means of accomplishing this two-fold goal is the competitive examination.

Exams are widely publicized throughout the nation. They may be administered for jobs in federal, state, city, municipal, town or village governments or agencies.

Any citizen may apply, with some limitations, such as the age or residence of applicants. Your experience and education may be reviewed to see whether you meet the requirements for the particular examination. When these requirements exist, they are reasonable and applied consistently to all applicants. Thus, a competitive examination may cause you some uneasiness now, but it is your privilege and safeguard.

C. *HOW ARE CIVIL SERVICE EXAMS DEVELOPED?*

Examinations are carefully written by trained technicians who are specialists in the field known as "psychological measurement," in consultation with recognized authorities in the field of work that the test will cover. These experts recommend the subject matter areas or skills to be tested; only those knowledges or skills important to your success on the job are included. The most reliable books and source materials available are used as references. Together, the experts and technicians judge the difficulty level of the questions.

Test technicians know how to phrase questions so that the problem is clearly stated. Their ethics do not permit "trick" or "catch" questions. Questions may have been tried out on sample groups, or subjected to statistical analysis, to determine their usefulness.

Written tests are often used in combination with performance tests, ratings of training and experience, and oral interviews. All of these measures combine to form the best-known means of finding the right person for the right job.

II. HOW TO PASS THE WRITTEN TEST

A. NATURE OF THE EXAMINATION

To prepare intelligently for civil service examinations, you should know how they differ from school examinations you have taken. In school you were assigned certain definite pages to read or subjects to cover. The examination questions were quite detailed and usually emphasized memory. Civil service exams, on the other hand, try to discover your present ability to perform the duties of a position, plus your potentiality to learn these duties. In other words, a civil service exam attempts to predict how successful you will be. Questions cover such a broad area that they cannot be as minute and detailed as school exam questions.

In the public service similar kinds of work, or positions, are grouped together in one "class." This process is known as *position-classification*. All the positions in a class are paid according to the salary range for that class. One class title covers all of these positions, and they are all tested by the same examination.

B. FOUR BASIC STEPS

1) Study the announcement

How, then, can you know what subjects to study? Our best answer is: "Learn as much as possible about the class of positions for which you've applied." The exam will test the knowledge, skills and abilities needed to do the work.

Your most valuable source of information about the position you want is the official exam announcement. This announcement lists the training and experience qualifications. Check these standards and apply only if you come reasonably close to meeting them.

The brief description of the position in the examination announcement offers some clues to the subjects which will be tested. Think about the job itself. Review the duties in your mind. Can you perform them, or are there some in which you are rusty? Fill in the blank spots in your preparation.

Many jurisdictions preview the written test in the exam announcement by including a section called "Knowledge and Abilities Required," "Scope of the Examination," or some similar heading. Here you will find out specifically what fields will be tested.

2) Review your own background

Once you learn in general what the position is all about, and what you need to know to do the work, ask yourself which subjects you already know fairly well and which need improvement. You may wonder whether to concentrate on improving your strong areas or on building some background in your fields of weakness. When the announcement has specified "some knowledge" or "considerable knowledge," or has used adjectives like "beginning principles of..." or "advanced ... methods," you can get a clue as to the number and difficulty of questions to be asked in any given field. More questions, and hence broader coverage, would be included for those subjects which are more important in the work. Now weigh your strengths and weaknesses against the job requirements and prepare accordingly.

3) Determine the level of the position

Another way to tell how intensively you should prepare is to understand the level of the job for which you are applying. Is it the entering level? In other words, is this the position in which beginners in a field of work are hired? Or is it an intermediate or advanced level? Sometimes this is indicated by such words as "Junior" or "Senior" in the class title. Other jurisdictions use Roman numerals to designate the level – Clerk I, Clerk II, for example. The word "Supervisor" sometimes appears in the title. If the level is not indicated by the title, check the description of duties. Will you be working under very close supervision, or will you have responsibility for independent decisions in this work?

4) Choose appropriate study materials

Now that you know the subjects to be examined and the relative amount of each subject to be covered, you can choose suitable study materials. For beginning level jobs, or even advanced ones, if you have a pronounced weakness in some aspect of your training, read a modern, standard textbook in that field. Be sure it is up to date and has general coverage. Such books are normally available at your library, and the librarian will be glad to help you locate one. For entry-level positions, questions of appropriate difficulty are chosen -- neither highly advanced questions, nor those too simple. Such questions require careful thought but not advanced training.

If the position for which you are applying is technical or advanced, you will read more advanced, specialized material. If you are already familiar with the basic principles of your field, elementary textbooks would waste your time. Concentrate on advanced textbooks and technical periodicals. Think through the concepts and review difficult problems in your field.

These are all general sources. You can get more ideas on your own initiative, following these leads. For example, training manuals and publications of the government agency which employs workers in your field can be useful, particularly for technical and professional positions. A letter or visit to the government department involved may result in more specific study suggestions, and certainly will provide you with a more definite idea of the exact nature of the position you are seeking.

III. KINDS OF TESTS

Tests are used for purposes other than measuring knowledge and ability to perform specified duties. For some positions, it is equally important to test ability to make adjustments to new situations or to profit from training. In others, basic mental abilities not dependent on information are essential. Questions which test these things may not appear as pertinent to the duties of the position as those which test for knowledge and information. Yet they are often highly important parts of a fair examination. For very general questions, it is almost impossible to help you direct your study efforts. What we can do is to point out some of the more common of these general abilities needed in public service positions and describe some typical questions.

1) General information

Broad, general information has been found useful for predicting job success in some kinds of work. This is tested in a variety of ways, from vocabulary lists to questions about current events. Basic background in some field of work, such as sociology or economics, may be sampled in a group of questions. Often these are principles which have become familiar to most persons through exposure rather than through formal training. It is difficult to advise you how to study for these questions; being alert to the world around you is our best suggestion.

2) Verbal ability

An example of an ability needed in many positions is verbal or language ability. Verbal ability is, in brief, the ability to use and understand words. Vocabulary and grammar tests are typical measures of this ability. Reading comprehension or paragraph interpretation questions are common in many kinds of civil service tests. You are given a paragraph of written material and asked to find its central meaning.

3) Numerical ability

Number skills can be tested by the familiar arithmetic problem, by checking paired lists of numbers to see which are alike and which are different, or by interpreting charts and graphs. In the latter test, a graph may be printed in the test booklet which you are asked to use as the basis for answering questions.

4) Observation

A popular test for law-enforcement positions is the observation test. A picture is shown to you for several minutes, then taken away. Questions about the picture test your ability to observe both details and larger elements.

5) Following directions

In many positions in the public service, the employee must be able to carry out written instructions dependably and accurately. You may be given a chart with several columns, each column listing a variety of information. The questions require you to carry out directions involving the information given in the chart.

6) Skills and aptitudes

Performance tests effectively measure some manual skills and aptitudes. When the skill is one in which you are trained, such as typing or shorthand, you can practice. These tests are often very much like those given in business school or high school courses. For many of the other skills and aptitudes, however, no short-time preparation can be made. Skills and abilities natural to you or that you have developed throughout your lifetime are being tested.

Many of the general questions just described provide all the data needed to answer the questions and ask you to use your reasoning ability to find the answers. Your best preparation for these tests, as well as for tests of facts and ideas, is to be at your physical and mental best. You, no doubt, have your own methods of getting into an exam-taking mood and keeping "in shape." The next section lists some ideas on this subject.

IV. KINDS OF QUESTIONS

Only rarely is the "essay" question, which you answer in narrative form, used in civil service tests. Civil service tests are usually of the short-answer type. Full instructions for answering these questions will be given to you at the examination. But in case this is your first experience with short-answer questions and separate answer sheets, here is what you need to know:

1) Multiple-choice Questions

Most popular of the short-answer questions is the "multiple choice" or "best answer" question. It can be used, for example, to test for factual knowledge, ability to solve problems or judgment in meeting situations found at work.

A multiple-choice question is normally one of three types—

- It can begin with an incomplete statement followed by several possible endings. You are to find the one ending which *best* completes the statement, although some of the others may not be entirely wrong.
- It can also be a complete statement in the form of a question which is answered by choosing one of the statements listed.

- It can be in the form of a problem – again you select the best answer.

Here is an example of a multiple-choice question with a discussion which should give you some clues as to the method for choosing the right answer:

When an employee has a complaint about his assignment, the action which will *best* help him overcome his difficulty is to
- A. discuss his difficulty with his coworkers
- B. take the problem to the head of the organization
- C. take the problem to the person who gave him the assignment
- D. say nothing to anyone about his complaint

In answering this question, you should study each of the choices to find which is best. Consider choice "A" – Certainly an employee may discuss his complaint with fellow employees, but no change or improvement can result, and the complaint remains unresolved. Choice "B" is a poor choice since the head of the organization probably does not know what assignment you have been given, and taking your problem to him is known as "going over the head" of the supervisor. The supervisor, or person who made the assignment, is the person who can clarify it or correct any injustice. Choice "C" is, therefore, correct. To say nothing, as in choice "D," is unwise. Supervisors have and interest in knowing the problems employees are facing, and the employee is seeking a solution to his problem.

2) True/False Questions

The "true/false" or "right/wrong" form of question is sometimes used. Here a complete statement is given. Your job is to decide whether the statement is right or wrong.

SAMPLE: A roaming cell-phone call to a nearby city costs less than a non-roaming call to a distant city.

This statement is wrong, or false, since roaming calls are more expensive.

This is not a complete list of all possible question forms, although most of the others are variations of these common types. You will always get complete directions for answering questions. Be sure you understand *how* to mark your answers – ask questions until you do.

V. RECORDING YOUR ANSWERS

Computer terminals are used more and more today for many different kinds of exams.

For an examination with very few applicants, you may be told to record your answers in the test booklet itself. Separate answer sheets are much more common. If this separate answer sheet is to be scored by machine – and this is often the case – it is highly important that you mark your answers correctly in order to get credit.

An electronic scoring machine is often used in civil service offices because of the speed with which papers can be scored. Machine-scored answer sheets must be marked with a pencil, which will be given to you. This pencil has a high graphite content which responds to the electronic scoring machine. As a matter of fact, stray dots may register as answers, so do not let your pencil rest on the answer sheet while you are pondering the correct answer. Also, if your pencil lead breaks or is otherwise defective, ask for another.

Since the answer sheet will be dropped in a slot in the scoring machine, be careful not to bend the corners or get the paper crumpled.

The answer sheet normally has five vertical columns of numbers, with 30 numbers to a column. These numbers correspond to the question numbers in your test booklet. After each number, going across the page are four or five pairs of dotted lines. These short dotted lines have small letters or numbers above them. The first two pairs may also have a "T" or "F" above the letters. This indicates that the first two pairs only are to be used if the questions are of the true-false type. If the questions are multiple choice, disregard the "T" and "F" and pay attention only to the small letters or numbers.

Answer your questions in the manner of the sample that follows:

32. The largest city in the United States is
    A. Washington, D.C.
    B. New York City
    C. Chicago
    D. Detroit
    E. San Francisco

1) Choose the answer you think is best. (New York City is the largest, so "B" is correct.)
2) Find the row of dotted lines numbered the same as the question you are answering. (Find row number 32)
3) Find the pair of dotted lines corresponding to the answer. (Find the pair of lines under the mark "B.")
4) Make a solid black mark between the dotted lines.

VI. BEFORE THE TEST

Common sense will help you find procedures to follow to get ready for an examination. Too many of us, however, overlook these sensible measures. Indeed, nervousness and fatigue have been found to be the most serious reasons why applicants fail to do their best on civil service tests. Here is a list of reminders:

- Begin your preparation early – Don't wait until the last minute to go scurrying around for books and materials or to find out what the position is all about.
- Prepare continuously – An hour a night for a week is better than an all-night cram session. This has been definitely established. What is more, a night a week for a month will return better dividends than crowding your study into a shorter period of time.
- Locate the place of the exam – You have been sent a notice telling you when and where to report for the examination. If the location is in a different town or otherwise unfamiliar to you, it would be well to inquire the best route and learn something about the building.
- Relax the night before the test – Allow your mind to rest. Do not study at all that night. Plan some mild recreation or diversion; then go to bed early and get a good night's sleep.
- Get up early enough to make a leisurely trip to the place for the test – This way unforeseen events, traffic snarls, unfamiliar buildings, etc. will not upset you.
- Dress comfortably – A written test is not a fashion show. You will be known by number and not by name, so wear something comfortable.

- Leave excess paraphernalia at home – Shopping bags and odd bundles will get in your way. You need bring only the items mentioned in the official notice you received; usually everything you need is provided. Do not bring reference books to the exam. They will only confuse those last minutes and be taken away from you when in the test room.
- Arrive somewhat ahead of time – If because of transportation schedules you must get there very early, bring a newspaper or magazine to take your mind off yourself while waiting.
- Locate the examination room – When you have found the proper room, you will be directed to the seat or part of the room where you will sit. Sometimes you are given a sheet of instructions to read while you are waiting. Do not fill out any forms until you are told to do so; just read them and be prepared.
- Relax and prepare to listen to the instructions
- If you have any physical problem that may keep you from doing your best, be sure to tell the test administrator. If you are sick or in poor health, you really cannot do your best on the exam. You can come back and take the test some other time.

VII. AT THE TEST

The day of the test is here and you have the test booklet in your hand. The temptation to get going is very strong. Caution! There is more to success than knowing the right answers. You must know how to identify your papers and understand variations in the type of short-answer question used in this particular examination. Follow these suggestions for maximum results from your efforts:

1) Cooperate with the monitor
The test administrator has a duty to create a situation in which you can be as much at ease as possible. He will give instructions, tell you when to begin, check to see that you are marking your answer sheet correctly, and so on. He is not there to guard you, although he will see that your competitors do not take unfair advantage. He wants to help you do your best.

2) Listen to all instructions
Don't jump the gun! Wait until you understand all directions. In most civil service tests you get more time than you need to answer the questions. So don't be in a hurry. Read each word of instructions until you clearly understand the meaning. Study the examples, listen to all announcements and follow directions. Ask questions if you do not understand what to do.

3) Identify your papers
Civil service exams are usually identified by number only. You will be assigned a number; you must not put your name on your test papers. Be sure to copy your number correctly. Since more than one exam may be given, copy your exact examination title.

4) Plan your time
Unless you are told that a test is a "speed" or "rate of work" test, speed itself is usually not important. Time enough to answer all the questions will be provided, but this does not mean that you have all day. An overall time limit has been set. Divide the total time (in minutes) by the number of questions to determine the approximate time you have for each question.

5) Do not linger over difficult questions

If you come across a difficult question, mark it with a paper clip (useful to have along) and come back to it when you have been through the booklet. One caution if you do this – be sure to skip a number on your answer sheet as well. Check often to be sure that you have not lost your place and that you are marking in the row numbered the same as the question you are answering.

6) Read the questions

Be sure you know what the question asks! Many capable people are unsuccessful because they failed to *read* the questions correctly.

7) Answer all questions

Unless you have been instructed that a penalty will be deducted for incorrect answers, it is better to guess than to omit a question.

8) Speed tests

It is often better NOT to guess on speed tests. It has been found that on timed tests people are tempted to spend the last few seconds before time is called in marking answers at random – without even reading them – in the hope of picking up a few extra points. To discourage this practice, the instructions may warn you that your score will be "corrected" for guessing. That is, a penalty will be applied. The incorrect answers will be deducted from the correct ones, or some other penalty formula will be used.

9) Review your answers

If you finish before time is called, go back to the questions you guessed or omitted to give them further thought. Review other answers if you have time.

10) Return your test materials

If you are ready to leave before others have finished or time is called, take ALL your materials to the monitor and leave quietly. Never take any test material with you. The monitor can discover whose papers are not complete, and taking a test booklet may be grounds for disqualification.

VIII. EXAMINATION TECHNIQUES

1) Read the general instructions carefully. These are usually printed on the first page of the exam booklet. As a rule, these instructions refer to the timing of the examination; the fact that you should not start work until the signal and must stop work at a signal, etc. If there are any *special* instructions, such as a choice of questions to be answered, make sure that you note this instruction carefully.

2) When you are ready to start work on the examination, that is as soon as the signal has been given, read the instructions to each question booklet, underline any key words or phrases, such as *least, best, outline, describe* and the like. In this way you will tend to answer as requested rather than discover on reviewing your paper that you *listed without describing*, that you selected the *worst* choice rather than the *best* choice, etc.

3) If the examination is of the objective or multiple-choice type – that is, each question will also give a series of possible answers: A, B, C or D, and you are called upon to select the best answer and write the letter next to that answer on your answer paper – it is advisable to start answering each question in turn. There may be anywhere from 50 to 100 such questions in the three or four hours allotted and you can see how much time would be taken if you read through all the questions before beginning to answer any. Furthermore, if you come across a question or group of questions which you know would be difficult to answer, it would undoubtedly affect your handling of all the other questions.

4) If the examination is of the essay type and contains but a few questions, it is a moot point as to whether you should read all the questions before starting to answer any one. Of course, if you are given a choice – say five out of seven and the like – then it is essential to read all the questions so you can eliminate the two that are most difficult. If, however, you are asked to answer all the questions, there may be danger in trying to answer the easiest one first because you may find that you will spend too much time on it. The best technique is to answer the first question, then proceed to the second, etc.

5) Time your answers. Before the exam begins, write down the time it started, then add the time allowed for the examination and write down the time it must be completed, then divide the time available somewhat as follows:
    - If 3-1/2 hours are allowed, that would be 210 minutes. If you have 80 objective-type questions, that would be an average of 2-1/2 minutes per question. Allow yourself no more than 2 minutes per question, or a total of 160 minutes, which will permit about 50 minutes to review.
    - If for the time allotment of 210 minutes there are 7 essay questions to answer, that would average about 30 minutes a question. Give yourself only 25 minutes per question so that you have about 35 minutes to review.

6) The most important instruction is to *read each question* and make sure you know what is wanted. The second most important instruction is to *time yourself properly* so that you answer every question. The third most important instruction is to *answer every question*. Guess if you have to but include something for each question. Remember that you will receive no credit for a blank and will probably receive some credit if you write something in answer to an essay question. If you guess a letter – say "B" for a multiple-choice question – you may have guessed right. If you leave a blank as an answer to a multiple-choice question, the examiners may respect your feelings but it will not add a point to your score. Some exams may penalize you for wrong answers, so in such cases *only*, you may not want to guess unless you have some basis for your answer.

7) Suggestions
    a. Objective-type questions
        1. Examine the question booklet for proper sequence of pages and questions
        2. Read all instructions carefully
        3. Skip any question which seems too difficult; return to it after all other questions have been answered
        4. Apportion your time properly; do not spend too much time on any single question or group of questions

5. Note and underline key words – *all, most, fewest, least, best, worst, same, opposite,* etc.
6. Pay particular attention to negatives
7. Note unusual option, e.g., unduly long, short, complex, different or similar in content to the body of the question
8. Observe the use of "hedging" words – *probably, may, most likely,* etc.
9. Make sure that your answer is put next to the same number as the question
10. Do not second-guess unless you have good reason to believe the second answer is definitely more correct
11. Cross out original answer if you decide another answer is more accurate; do not erase until you are ready to hand your paper in
12. Answer all questions; guess unless instructed otherwise
13. Leave time for review

b. Essay questions
  1. Read each question carefully
  2. Determine exactly what is wanted. Underline key words or phrases.
  3. Decide on outline or paragraph answer
  4. Include many different points and elements unless asked to develop any one or two points or elements
  5. Show impartiality by giving pros and cons unless directed to select one side only
  6. Make and write down any assumptions you find necessary to answer the questions
  7. Watch your English, grammar, punctuation and choice of words
  8. Time your answers; don't crowd material

8) Answering the essay question

Most essay questions can be answered by framing the specific response around several key words or ideas. Here are a few such key words or ideas:

M's: manpower, materials, methods, money, management
P's: purpose, program, policy, plan, procedure, practice, problems, pitfalls, personnel, public relations

  a. Six basic steps in handling problems:
    1. Preliminary plan and background development
    2. Collect information, data and facts
    3. Analyze and interpret information, data and facts
    4. Analyze and develop solutions as well as make recommendations
    5. Prepare report and sell recommendations
    6. Install recommendations and follow up effectiveness

  b. Pitfalls to avoid
    1. *Taking things for granted* – A statement of the situation does not necessarily imply that each of the elements is necessarily true; for example, a complaint may be invalid and biased so that all that can be taken for granted is that a complaint has been registered

2. *Considering only one side of a situation* – Wherever possible, indicate several alternatives and then point out the reasons you selected the best one
3. *Failing to indicate follow up* – Whenever your answer indicates action on your part, make certain that you will take proper follow-up action to see how successful your recommendations, procedures or actions turn out to be
4. *Taking too long in answering any single question* – Remember to time your answers properly

IX. AFTER THE TEST

Scoring procedures differ in detail among civil service jurisdictions although the general principles are the same. Whether the papers are hand-scored or graded by machine we have described, they are nearly always graded by number. That is, the person who marks the paper knows only the number – never the name – of the applicant. Not until all the papers have been graded will they be matched with names. If other tests, such as training and experience or oral interview ratings have been given, scores will be combined. Different parts of the examination usually have different weights. For example, the written test might count 60 percent of the final grade, and a rating of training and experience 40 percent. In many jurisdictions, veterans will have a certain number of points added to their grades.

After the final grade has been determined, the names are placed in grade order and an eligible list is established. There are various methods for resolving ties between those who get the same final grade – probably the most common is to place first the name of the person whose application was received first. Job offers are made from the eligible list in the order the names appear on it. You will be notified of your grade and your rank as soon as all these computations have been made. This will be done as rapidly as possible.

People who are found to meet the requirements in the announcement are called "eligibles." Their names are put on a list of eligible candidates. An eligible's chances of getting a job depend on how high he stands on this list and how fast agencies are filling jobs from the list.

When a job is to be filled from a list of eligibles, the agency asks for the names of people on the list of eligibles for that job. When the civil service commission receives this request, it sends to the agency the names of the three people highest on this list. Or, if the job to be filled has specialized requirements, the office sends the agency the names of the top three persons who meet these requirements from the general list.

The appointing officer makes a choice from among the three people whose names were sent to him. If the selected person accepts the appointment, the names of the others are put back on the list to be considered for future openings.

That is the rule in hiring from all kinds of eligible lists, whether they are for typist, carpenter, chemist, or something else. For every vacancy, the appointing officer has his choice of any one of the top three eligibles on the list. This explains why the person whose name is on top of the list sometimes does not get an appointment when some of the persons lower on the list do. If the appointing officer chooses the second or third eligible, the No. 1 eligible does not get a job at once, but stays on the list until he is appointed or the list is terminated.

X. HOW TO PASS THE INTERVIEW TEST

The examination for which you applied requires an oral interview test. You have already taken the written test and you are now being called for the interview test – the final part of the formal examination.

You may think that it is not possible to prepare for an interview test and that there are no procedures to follow during an interview. Our purpose is to point out some things you can do in advance that will help you and some good rules to follow and pitfalls to avoid while you are being interviewed.

What is an interview supposed to test?

The written examination is designed to test the technical knowledge and competence of the candidate; the oral is designed to evaluate intangible qualities, not readily measured otherwise, and to establish a list showing the relative fitness of each candidate – as measured against his competitors – for the position sought. Scoring is not on the basis of "right" and "wrong," but on a sliding scale of values ranging from "not passable" to "outstanding." As a matter of fact, it is possible to achieve a relatively low score without a single "incorrect" answer because of evident weakness in the qualities being measured.

Occasionally, an examination may consist entirely of an oral test – either an individual or a group oral. In such cases, information is sought concerning the technical knowledges and abilities of the candidate, since there has been no written examination for this purpose. More commonly, however, an oral test is used to supplement a written examination.

Who conducts interviews?

The composition of oral boards varies among different jurisdictions. In nearly all, a representative of the personnel department serves as chairman. One of the members of the board may be a representative of the department in which the candidate would work. In some cases, "outside experts" are used, and, frequently, a businessman or some other representative of the general public is asked to serve. Labor and management or other special groups may be represented. The aim is to secure the services of experts in the appropriate field.

However the board is composed, it is a good idea (and not at all improper or unethical) to ascertain in advance of the interview who the members are and what groups they represent. When you are introduced to them, you will have some idea of their backgrounds and interests, and at least you will not stutter and stammer over their names.

What should be done before the interview?

While knowledge about the board members is useful and takes some of the surprise element out of the interview, there is other preparation which is more substantive. It *is* possible to prepare for an oral interview – in several ways:

1) Keep a copy of your application and review it carefully before the interview

This may be the only document before the oral board, and the starting point of the interview. Know what education and experience you have listed there, and the sequence and dates of all of it. Sometimes the board will ask you to review the highlights of your experience for them; you should not have to hem and haw doing it.

2) Study the class specification and the examination announcement

Usually, the oral board has one or both of these to guide them. The qualities, characteristics or knowledges required by the position sought are stated in these documents. They offer valuable clues as to the nature of the oral interview. For example, if the job involves supervisory responsibilities, the announcement will usually indicate that knowledge of modern supervisory methods and the qualifications of the candidate as a supervisor will be tested. If so, you can expect such questions, frequently in the form of a hypothetical situation which you are expected to solve. NEVER go into an oral without knowledge of the duties and responsibilities of the job you seek.

3) Think through each qualification required

Try to visualize the kind of questions you would ask if you were a board member. How well could you answer them? Try especially to appraise your own knowledge and background in each area, *measured against the job sought*, and identify any areas in which you are weak. Be critical and realistic – do not flatter yourself.

4) Do some general reading in areas in which you feel you may be weak

For example, if the job involves supervision and your past experience has NOT, some general reading in supervisory methods and practices, particularly in the field of human relations, might be useful. Do NOT study agency procedures or detailed manuals. The oral board will be testing your understanding and capacity, not your memory.

5) Get a good night's sleep and watch your general health and mental attitude

You will want a clear head at the interview. Take care of a cold or any other minor ailment, and of course, no hangovers.

What should be done on the day of the interview?

Now comes the day of the interview itself. Give yourself plenty of time to get there. Plan to arrive somewhat ahead of the scheduled time, particularly if your appointment is in the fore part of the day. If a previous candidate fails to appear, the board might be ready for you a bit early. By early afternoon an oral board is almost invariably behind schedule if there are many candidates, and you may have to wait. Take along a book or magazine to read, or your application to review, but leave any extraneous material in the waiting room when you go in for your interview. In any event, relax and compose yourself.

The matter of dress is important. The board is forming impressions about you – from your experience, your manners, your attitude, and your appearance. Give your personal appearance careful attention. Dress your best, but not your flashiest. Choose conservative, appropriate clothing, and be sure it is immaculate. This is a business interview, and your appearance should indicate that you regard it as such. Besides, being well groomed and properly dressed will help boost your confidence.

Sooner or later, someone will call your name and escort you into the interview room. *This is it.* From here on you are on your own. It is too late for any more preparation. But remember, you asked for this opportunity to prove your fitness, and you are here because your request was granted.

What happens when you go in?

The usual sequence of events will be as follows: The clerk (who is often the board stenographer) will introduce you to the chairman of the oral board, who will introduce you to the other members of the board. Acknowledge the introductions before you sit down. Do not be surprised if you find a microphone facing you or a stenotypist sitting by. Oral interviews are usually recorded in the event of an appeal or other review.

Usually the chairman of the board will open the interview by reviewing the highlights of your education and work experience from your application – primarily for the benefit of the other members of the board, as well as to get the material into the record. Do not interrupt or comment unless there is an error or significant misinterpretation; if that is the case, do not hesitate. But do not quibble about insignificant matters. Also, he will usually ask you some question about your education, experience or your present job – partly to get you to start talking and to establish the interviewing "rapport." He may start the actual questioning, or turn it over to one of the other members. Frequently, each member undertakes the questioning on a particular area, one in which he is perhaps most competent, so you can expect each member to participate in the examination. Because time is limited, you may also expect some rather abrupt switches in the direction the questioning takes, so do not be upset by it. Normally, a board member will not pursue a single line of questioning unless he discovers a particular strength or weakness.

After each member has participated, the chairman will usually ask whether any member has any further questions, then will ask you if you have anything you wish to add. Unless you are expecting this question, it may floor you. Worse, it may start you off on an extended, extemporaneous speech. The board is not usually seeking more information. The question is principally to offer you a last opportunity to present further qualifications or to indicate that you have nothing to add. So, if you feel that a significant qualification or characteristic has been overlooked, it is proper to point it out in a sentence or so. Do not compliment the board on the thoroughness of their examination – they have been sketchy, and you know it. If you wish, merely say, "No thank you, I have nothing further to add." This is a point where you can "talk yourself out" of a good impression or fail to present an important bit of information. Remember, *you close the interview yourself*.

The chairman will then say, "That is all, Mr. _____, thank you." Do not be startled; the interview is over, and quicker than you think. Thank him, gather your belongings and take your leave. Save your sigh of relief for the other side of the door.

How to put your best foot forward

Throughout this entire process, you may feel that the board individually and collectively is trying to pierce your defenses, seek out your hidden weaknesses and embarrass and confuse you. Actually, this is not true. They are obliged to make an appraisal of your qualifications for the job you are seeking, and they want to see you in your best light. Remember, they must interview all candidates and a non-cooperative candidate may become a failure in spite of their best efforts to bring out his qualifications. Here are 15 suggestions that will help you:

1) Be natural – Keep your attitude confident, not cocky

If you are not confident that you can do the job, do not expect the board to be. Do not apologize for your weaknesses, try to bring out your strong points. The board is interested in a positive, not negative, presentation. Cockiness will antagonize any board member and make him wonder if you are covering up a weakness by a false show of strength.

2) Get comfortable, but don't lounge or sprawl

Sit erectly but not stiffly. A careless posture may lead the board to conclude that you are careless in other things, or at least that you are not impressed by the importance of the occasion. Either conclusion is natural, even if incorrect. Do not fuss with your clothing, a pencil or an ashtray. Your hands may occasionally be useful to emphasize a point; do not let them become a point of distraction.

3) Do not wisecrack or make small talk

This is a serious situation, and your attitude should show that you consider it as such. Further, the time of the board is limited – they do not want to waste it, and neither should you.

4) Do not exaggerate your experience or abilities
   In the first place, from information in the application or other interviews and sources, the board may know more about you than you think. Secondly, you probably will not get away with it. An experienced board is rather adept at spotting such a situation, so do not take the chance.

5) If you know a board member, do not make a point of it, yet do not hide it
   Certainly you are not fooling him, and probably not the other members of the board. Do not try to take advantage of your acquaintanceship – it will probably do you little good.

6) Do not dominate the interview
   Let the board do that. They will give you the clues – do not assume that you have to do all the talking. Realize that the board has a number of questions to ask you, and do not try to take up all the interview time by showing off your extensive knowledge of the answer to the first one.

7) Be attentive
   You only have 20 minutes or so, and you should keep your attention at its sharpest throughout. When a member is addressing a problem or question to you, give him your undivided attention. Address your reply principally to him, but do not exclude the other board members.

8) Do not interrupt
   A board member may be stating a problem for you to analyze. He will ask you a question when the time comes. Let him state the problem, and wait for the question.

9) Make sure you understand the question
   Do not try to answer until you are sure what the question is. If it is not clear, restate it in your own words or ask the board member to clarify it for you. However, do not haggle about minor elements.

10) Reply promptly but not hastily
   A common entry on oral board rating sheets is "candidate responded readily," or "candidate hesitated in replies." Respond as promptly and quickly as you can, but do not jump to a hasty, ill-considered answer.

11) Do not be peremptory in your answers
   A brief answer is proper – but do not fire your answer back. That is a losing game from your point of view. The board member can probably ask questions much faster than you can answer them.

12) Do not try to create the answer you think the board member wants
   He is interested in what kind of mind you have and how it works – not in playing games. Furthermore, he can usually spot this practice and will actually grade you down on it.

13) Do not switch sides in your reply merely to agree with a board member
   Frequently, a member will take a contrary position merely to draw you out and to see if you are willing and able to defend your point of view. Do not start a debate, yet do not surrender a good position. If a position is worth taking, it is worth defending.

14) Do not be afraid to admit an error in judgment if you are shown to be wrong

The board knows that you are forced to reply without any opportunity for careful consideration. Your answer may be demonstrably wrong. If so, admit it and get on with the interview.

15) Do not dwell at length on your present job

The opening question may relate to your present assignment. Answer the question but do not go into an extended discussion. You are being examined for a *new* job, not your present one. As a matter of fact, try to phrase ALL your answers in terms of the job for which you are being examined.

Basis of Rating

Probably you will forget most of these "do's" and "don'ts" when you walk into the oral interview room. Even remembering them all will not ensure you a passing grade. Perhaps you did not have the qualifications in the first place. But remembering them will help you to put your best foot forward, without treading on the toes of the board members.

Rumor and popular opinion to the contrary notwithstanding, an oral board wants you to make the best appearance possible. They know you are under pressure – but they also want to see how you respond to it as a guide to what your reaction would be under the pressures of the job you seek. They will be influenced by the degree of poise you display, the personal traits you show and the manner in which you respond.

ABOUT THIS BOOK

This book contains tests divided into Examination Sections. Go through each test, answering every question in the margin. We have also attached a sample answer sheet at the back of the book that can be removed and used. At the end of each test look at the answer key and check your answers. On the ones you got wrong, look at the right answer choice and learn. Do not fill in the answers first. Do not memorize the questions and answers, but understand the answer and principles involved. On your test, the questions will likely be different from the samples. Questions are changed and new ones added. If you understand these past questions you should have success with any changes that arise. Tests may consist of several types of questions. We have additional books on each subject should more study be advisable or necessary for you. Finally, the more you study, the better prepared you will be. This book is intended to be the last thing you study before you walk into the examination room. Prior study of relevant texts is also recommended. NLC publishes some of these in our Fundamental Series. Knowledge and good sense are important factors in passing your exam. Good luck also helps. So now study this Passbook, absorb the material contained within and take that knowledge into the examination. Then do your best to pass that exam.

EXAMINATION SECTION

EXAMINATION SECTION
TEST 1

DIRECTIONS: Answer the following questions directly, briefly, and succinctly.

1. What is the usual number of threads per inch on a screw stay bolt?

2. What is the apparatus which enables the steam pressure to be used in forcing feed water into a five-horsepower boiler?

3. What is the rule for the test pressure in a hydrostatic test on a stationary boiler?

4. What is used to hold plates on the bending block?

5. Where is a ferrule placed?

6. What swaging tool is used to form a rolled edge on the end of boiler tubes?

7. What is the joint called that is made by placing the edges seam to seam and covering with a narrow strip or strap?

8. What is the distance called between rivet centers measured along direction of seam?

KEY (CORRECT ANSWERS)

1. 10 to 14

2. Injector (inspirator) pump

3. $1\frac{1}{4}$ times working pressure to 2 times pressure ($1\frac{1}{4}$ to 2 times boiler rating)
   25% ($\frac{1}{4}$) above pressure to 100% above pressure

4. Clamps
   Dogs
   Pines (pegs) (stops)

5. Around tube (around flue)
   End of tube (where tube is broken)
   In tube (in flue) hole
   In flue (tube) (crown) sheet

6. Beading tool
   Belling (bell) tool
   Flaring tool

7. Butt strap
   Butt seam
   Butt
   Square

8. Pitch
   Spacing

TEST 2

DIRECTIONS: Answer the following questions directly, briefly, and succinctly.

1. How much does the tube project beyond the tube sheet after setting?
2. What is the hole called that is drilled in the end of a stay bolt?
3. What is the kind of boiler called where the tubes of water are surrounded by the fire?
4. What is another name for a fusible plug?
5. What is used on gaskets to prevent sticking?
6. How does one fasten the end of a tube in a fire tube boiler?
7. What usually causes a boiler to *bag* in spots?
8. About how much larger are the holes for tubes than the tubes themselves?

KEY (CORRECT ANSWERS)

1. 3/16" to 1/2"

2. Telltale (tattletale)
   Test hole
   Safety hole

3. Water tube

4. Safety
   Soft
   Low water

5. Graphite
   Plumbago

6. Roll and bead it
   Bead
   Roll it (rolling)
   Expand (with expander)

7. Scale (mud) (dirt) (grease) (oil)
   Low water (lack of water)
   Broken stay bolts (broken bolts)
   Corrosion (pitted)
   Overheat (excessive heat)

8. 1/32
   1/16
   3/32
   1/8

TEST 3

DIRECTIONS: Answer the following questions directly, briefly, and succinctly.

1. From what part of the furnace do gases enter the radiator?
2. What kind of joint acts as a stiffener in the run of a large duct?
3. What machine is used to make an edge on a sheet-metal disc?
4. What should be installed in each leader run?
5. What is the part of a cast-iron furnace called which rests on top of the combustion chamber?
6. What gauge galvanized iron is usually used for large-sized angles?
7. What is the part of a cast-iron furnace called that rests on top of the firepot?
8. What does C.F.M. mean?
9. What is the enlarged piece of pipe called that is placed on the bottom end of the riser?
10. What is the short pieces of pipe called which fit into the hood of the furnace?

2 (#3)

KEY (CORRECT ANSWERS)

1. Combustion chamber (dome)

2. Standing seam
   Lock strip (double lock)
   S-slip (slip)

3. Edger (thick edge machine)
   Beader
   Flanger
   Burring machine
   Crimper

4. Damper

5. Radiator

6. 22 to 28 gauge

7. Combustion chamber (dome)

8. Cubic feet per minute

9. Boot

10. Collars

TEST 4

DIRECTIONS: Answer the following questions directly, briefly, and succinctly.

1. What is the openings in the cupola called through which air is blown?
2. What material makes up the cupola bottom?
3. By what means can one tell when the cupola bed is ready for the charge?
4. What name is given to the bottom part of the cupola where the molten metal collects?
5. What is another name for the trough that runs from the tap hole to the catch ladle?
6. What stone is put into the charge as a purifier?
7. What is the chamber around the cupola called through which air goes to the tuyeres?
8. What is the clay ball called that is used to stop up the tap hole?
9. What is run to the bottom of the cupola when all the iron has run out?
10. What is the section of the cupola called where the tap hole is located?
11. What content is pig iron classified by?
12. What is the section of the cupola called directly above the tuyere zone?
13. What tool is used to open the tap hole?
14. What will happen to the molten metal if the tap hole in the breast is too long?
15. What is the first charge of coke called that is put into the cupola?

KEY (CORRECT ANSWERS)

1. Tuyeres

2. Sand

3. Color (cherry red)
   When coke is burned through

4. Basin (bed) (reservoir) (bosch)

5. Spout

6. Limestone

7. Wind box (blast belt)

8. Bott (bod)
   Stopper
   Plug

9. Drop (pull) (knock out) (dump)

10. Breast

11. Silicon (silica) (si)

12. Melting zone (melting point)

13. Tapping bar (tapping rod)

14. Freeze (chill) (harden)

15. Bed charge (ground charge)

TEST 5

DIRECTIONS: Answer the following questions directly, briefly, and succinctly.

1. Where should a crucible be put to cool off?
2. What is used to remove the crucible from the furnace?
3. What material is used to make a mixture for repairing cracks and worn spots in the lining of a melting furnace?
4. What instrument is used to measure the temperature of molten metal in the furnace?
5. What is added to a brass mixture to make it flow more freely?
6. Why should aluminum NOT be overheated?
7. What is meant by the expression, *85 and three 5's*?
8. What is a furnace tilted with?
9. In what part of the furnace is a tilting furnace charged?
10. What two metals are used to make up yellow brass?
11. What alloys are used in making lightweight castings?
12. For what purpose does the furnace swing back and forth?
13. How many degrees of heat are required to melt aluminum?
14. By what means can one tell when the brass in the crucible is ready to pour?
15. What flux is used to form slag when melting brass?

2 (#5)

KEY (CORRECT ANSWERS)

1. Warm place
   In or near furnace

2. Tongs
   Chain hooks

3. Fire clay (fire cement) (furnace cement)
   Canister
   Carborundum and fire sand

4. Pyrometer

5. Phosphor copper (phosphorus)

6. Takes up gas (oxidizes) (burns)

7. 85% copper, 5% lead, 5% tin, and 5% zinc
   Red brass

8. Handwheel (wheel)
   Worn gear (teeth)

9. Charging door
   Top

10. Copper
    Zinc

11. Aluminum
    Brass

12. Divide heat evenly
    Mix metals thoroughly
    Make pouring easy

13. 1,000 degrees to 1,300 degrees

14. Color
    Temperature (pyrometer)

15. Glass
    Sand
    Borax
    Soda (soda ash)

TEST 6

DIRECTIONS: Answer the following questions directly, briefly, and succinctly.

1. Why can you NOT make an alloy of copper and tin by placing both metals in the crucible and melting them together?

2. How are crucibles sometimes broken during charging?

3. Why should a crucible be annealed before using?

4. How are the sizes of crucibles indicated?

5. In making brass, which metal is melted FIRST?

6. What is the difference between red brass and yellow brass?

7. What instrument is used to measure the temperature of melted metal?

8. What is used to carry the crucible to the mold?

9. What is put into molten metal to purify it?

10. If brass is held over in the furnace after the proper pouring temperature has been reached, what happens to the zinc?

KEY (CORRECT ANSWERS)

1. Tin would burn up (lose the tin)
   Tin melts at lower temperature
   Won't mix right
   Difference in melting point

2. Dropping ingots in (throwing in metal)
   Wedging metal into it (metal is too tight)
   Rough handling (hitting) (poking)
   Putting cold piece into a hot pot

3. Prevent cracking (prevent breaking) (prevent bursting)
   Remove moisture (remove dampness) (dry out)

4. By numbers (10, 50, 70, 150, etc.)

5. Copper

6. Red has more copper
   Red has tin
   Yellow has more zinc (zinc content)
   Yellow has less tin (yellow has no tin)

7. Pyrometer

8. Shank (bale)
   Tongs

9. Flux
   Phosphorus (phosphor content)
   Charcoal
   Glass
   Borax

10. Burns out (oxidizes) (goes off in smoke) (evaporates)

TEST 7

DIRECTIONS: Answer the following questions directly, briefly, and succinctly.

1. Why should bricks not be placed too far apart in a lining?

2. What is the scrap metal reclaimed from machinings called?

3. What is glass in a crucible used for?

4. What type of casting MUST the metal be very fluid for?

5. Of what material are pots made?

KEY (CORRECT ANSWERS)

1. Burns through (burns outside case of furnace)
   Lining burns (falls) out (fire clay comes out)
   Lose heat (heat escapes)

2. Borings
   Turnings (shavings)

3. Prevent oxidizing (burning) of metal
   To cover metal (keeps air from metal)
   Keeps gas from forming
   Collects slag (dress) over top
   To clean metal (to purify)

4. Small
   Thin
   Light

5. Graphite (plumbago)
   Fire-clay (clay)
   Silicon carbide (carborundum) T
   Ter-cod (Terra-cotta)

EXAMINATION SECTION
TEST 1

DIRECTIONS: Each question or incomplete statement is followed by several suggested answers or completions. Select the one that BEST answers the question or completes the statement. *PRINT THE LETTER OF THE CORRECT ANSWER IN THE SPACE AT THE RIGHT.*

1. A steam heating boiler is classified as a low pressure boiler when it generates steam at a gage pressure of   1.____

   A. not more than 30 pounds per square inch
   B. not more than 25 pounds per square inch
   C. not more than 20 pounds per square inch
   D. 15 pounds per square inch or less

2. A hot water heating boiler is classified as a low pressure boiler when it produces hot water at a gage pressure   2.____

   A. not more than 200 pounds per square inch
   B. not more than 175 pounds per square inch
   C. not more than 160 pounds per square inch
   D. equal to an absolute pressure of 200 pounds per square inch

3. Of the following processes, the one which is NOT involved in the transfer of heat in a boiler from the hot gases to the water is   3.____

   A. radiation   B. conduction
   C. convection   D. evaporation

4. The MINIMUM flue gas CO_2 reading permitted in a large metropolitan city is   4.____

   A. 5%   B. 8%   C. 12%   D. 16%

5. The Ringelmann Chart is a device that is used for checking   5.____

   A. smoke density from a chimney
   B. boiler water condition
   C. percent CO_2 of the flue gas
   D. the carbon content of coal

6. Low voltage control circuits for oil burners usually operate at a voltage of _____ volts.   6.____

   A. six (6)   B. twelve (12)
   C. twenty-five (25)   D. fifty (50)

7. The connection known as a *Hartford Loop* is usually found on   7.____

   A. radiators
   B. high pressure hot water heaters
   C. low pressure unit heaters
   D. low pressure steam boilers

8. Of the following types of fuel oils, the one that has the GREATEST heat value per gallon is _____ oil.

    A. diesel   B. #2   C. #4   D. #6

9. Of the following types of fuel, the one which has the HIGHEST heat content per pound (Btu/lb) is

    A. #2 fuel oil
    B. semibituminous coal
    C. semianthracite coal
    D. wood

10. The atomization of oil in the average domestic gun-type burner is accomplished by the

    A. air pressure
    B. pressure and centrifugal action of the oil
    C. low steam pressure
    D. draft effect of the stack

11. The type of fuel oil pump MOST commonly used with gun-type oil burners is the _____ type.

    A. centrifugal
    B. external or internal gear
    C. volute
    D. propeller

12. Chimney draft is usually measured in

    A. inches of mercury
    B. inches of water
    C. feet of water
    D. pounds per square inch

13. *Draft* that is produced over the fire or in a chimney without the use of any mechanical aids is generally known as _____ draft.

    A. balanced
    B. induced
    C. positive
    D. natural

14. Assume that a residential heating control system consists of a room thermostat, a limit control, a combustion control, a safety control, and a control relay. These controls would MOST likely be used with

    A. automatic gas-fired burners
    B. automatic oil-fired burners
    C. coal-fired stokers
    D. electric heating systems

15. A gauge that can be used for measuring either a vacuum or positive pressure in pounds per square inch is generally called a _____ gauge.

    A. compound
    B. pressure
    C. boiler
    D. vacuum

16. The purpose of a goose-neck connection to a Bourdon type steam gage is to

    A. prevent water getting into the gage tube
    B. prevent steam getting into the gage tube
    C. correct for trapped air in the line
    D. allow impurities to settle in the tube

17. The device that is generally used to reduce high pressure steam to low pressure steam is called a   17.____

    A. pressure relief valve
    B. pressure regulating valve
    C. condenser
    D. by-pass control valve

18. The MAXIMUM size of boiler safety valve that can be used on a low pressure boiler is   18.____

    A. 2"   B. $3\frac{1}{2}"$ C. $4\frac{1}{2}"$ D. $5\frac{1}{2}"$

19. If the water level in a steam heating boiler is unsteady, the probable cause may MOST likely be due to   19.____

    A. overfiring of boiler
    B. the use of a poor grade of fuel
    C. insufficient radiation in the heating system
    D. the use of an oversized boiler

20. The PRIMARY reason for using a gate valve in low pressure steam lines is to   20.____

    A. vary the steam pressure
    B. allow for quick opening
    C. reduce the flow of condensate to the boiler
    D. allow full free flow

21. Of the following types of valves, the one which is generally used to allow fluids to flow in one direction only is the   21.____

    A. gas cock   B. globe valve
    C. check valve   D. by-pass valve

22. The type of valve that is usually in a line with a swing check valve is a _____ valve.   22.____

    A. gate   B. diaphragm
    C. quick opening   D. globe

23. Excessive use of highly alkaline water in a boiler would probably result in boiler   23.____

    A. caustic embrittlement   B. priming
    C. foaming   D. corrosion

24. In a fire tube boiler, most of the soot usually accumulates   24.____

    A. on the inside surface of the tubes
    B. on the bridge wall
    C. in the combustion chamber
    D. on the outside surface of the tubes

25. Pneumatic tools are usually operated by   25.____

    A. steam   B. air   C. water   D. electricity

26. An *intercooler* is a device usually used in conjunction with a(n)

   A. boiler
   B. gear type oil pump
   C. centrifugal water pump
   D. air compressor

27. Of the following types of boilers, the one that is MOST commonly used for low pressure steam operation is the _____ boiler.

   A. Stirling
   B. cross-drum straight-tube
   C. cast iron vertical header logitudinal
   D. fire tube

28. The sum of the following pipe lengths, 15 5/8", 8 3/4", 30 5/6", and 20 1/2", is *most nearly*

   A. 77 1/8"   B. 76 3/16"   C. 75 3/16"   D. 74 5/16"

29. A boiler shell can sometimes be repaired temporarily by means of a

   A. soft patch and patch bolt
   B. hard patch and cap screws
   C. hard patch and rivets
   D. soft patch and rivets

30. The method generally used to provide rigidity for the internal flat surfaces of horizontal fire tube boilers is by

   A. riveting   B. staying   C. welding   D. caulking

31. The function of try-cocks on a boiler is PRIMARILY to

   A. drain the gage glass
   B. add water to the boiler
   C. check the gage glass reading
   D. blow down the water column

32. A boiler *blow-off* is usually connected

   A. to the steam compartment of the boiler
   B. next to the water column
   C. to the lowest water space available
   D. to the Hartford Loop

33. A boiler feedwater regulator automatically controls the

   A. water temperature in the boiler
   B. water pressure to the boiler
   C. feedwater treatment to the boiler
   D. water supply to the boiler

34. A feedwater heater in a steam generating plant is generally used to

   A. heat and condition water to the boiler
   B. provide make-up steam for the boiler
   C. feed hot water to plumbing fixtures
   D. increase feedwater pressure

35. If the outside diameter of a pipe is 6 inches and the wall thickness is $\frac{1}{2}$ inch, the inside area of this pipe, in square inches, is *most nearly*

    A. 15.7   B. 17.3   C. 19.6   D. 23.8

36. The type of pipe, used for water or gas, that should NOT be welded is _____ pipe.

    A. galvanized
    B. brass
    C. black wrought iron
    D. black steel

37. The instrument usually used to calibrate steam pressure gages is known as a _____ tester.

    A. lever-arm weight
    B. dead-weight
    C. Fyrite
    D. calibrated spring scale

38. A boiler horsepower is the evaporation from and at 212°F of _____ pounds of water per hour.

    A. 34.50   B. 30.50   C. 29.50   D. 25.50

39. A steam heating system that operates under both vacuum and low pressure conditions without use of a vacuum pump is known as a _____ system.

    A. forced return
    B. low pressure
    C. vacuum
    D. vapor

40. The purpose of an expansion tank in a hot water heating system is to

    A. add cold water to the system when needed
    B. prevent water hammer in the system
    C. allow for changes in the volume of water in the system
    D. store the water of the system when boiler is off the line

KEY (CORRECT ANSWERS)

1.	D	11.	B	21.	C	31.	C
2.	C	12.	B	22.	A	32.	C
3.	D	13.	D	23.	A	33.	D
4.	B	14.	B	24.	A	34.	A
5.	A	15.	A	25.	B	35.	C
6.	C	16.	B	26.	D	36.	A
7.	D	17.	B	27.	D	37.	B
8.	D	18.	C	28.	C	38.	A
9.	A	19.	A	29.	A	39.	D
10.	B	20.	D	30.	B	40.	C

TEST 2

DIRECTIONS: Each question or incomplete statement is followed by several suggested answers or completions. Select the one that BEST answers the question or completes the statement. *PRINT THE LETTER OF THE CORRECT ANSWER IN THE SPACE AT THE RIGHT.*

1. The pressure relief valve in a forced hot water heating system is generally mounted　　1.____

   A. on top of the boiler
   B. on top of the air cushion tank
   C. in the hot water return line
   D. on the line between the circulating pump and the boiler

2. In a forced hot water circulating system, the circulating pump is usually controlled by a　　2.____

   A. low-water cut out   B. room thermostat
   C. return-pump control   D. float

3. The diameter of a roof vent from an open expansion tank in a hot water heating system should be NOT less than　　3.____

   A. 5"   B. 4"   C. 3"   D. 2"

4. If the circumference of a circle measures 12.566 inches, its diameter is equal to *most nearly*　　4.____

   A. 2.75"   B. 3.00"   C. 3.50"   D. 4.00"

5. A valve that opens when its solenoid is energized and closes when the current is interrupted is known as a _____ valve.　　5.____

   A. magnetic   B. thermostatic
   C. relay   D. shut-off

6. The device that shuts off the flow of fuel oil to a rotary cup type oil burner, in case of primary air failure, is generally known as a　　6.____

   A. flame supervisor   B. pressuretrol
   C. aquastat   D. vaporstat

7. A device used to assure a proper temperature of No. 6 fuel oil before it is allowed to enter a burner is known as a　　7.____

   A. thermostat   B. aquastat
   C. pyrostat   D. fustat

8. A device used to start the operation of line voltage equipment by means of a low voltage control circuit is called a　　8.____

   A. circuit breaker   B. relay
   C. rectifier   D. variac

9. A pyrometer is generally used to measure the　　9.____

   A. specific gravity of a liquid
   B. density of a gas

20

C. temperature of flue gas
D. percent of carbon dioxide

10. A low water cut-off on a boiler is usually operated by means of a

    A. bellows   B. helix   C. float   D. diaphragm

11. Assume that the water level in the gauge glass of a steaming boiler drops out of sight during a test of the low water cut-off.
    As an inspector, you

    A. order the boiler to be taken off the line
    B. assume the cut-off is working properly
    C. order more water to be put into the boiler
    D. order the drain valves to be opened immediately

12. The function of a *pressuretrol* on an oil-fired steam boiler is to keep the

    A. oil pressure constant
    B. steam pressure from exceeding a predetermined amount
    C. water pressure above 20 pounds per square inch
    D. draft pressure below atmosphere

13. A *remote control switch* for an oil burner should usually be located

    A. next to the three-way magnetic oil valve
    B. only at the boiler
    C. at the exit of the boiler room
    D. in the superintendent's office

14. A stack switch is a device that is used to shut off the oil burner in case of

    A. flame failure
    B. high steam pressure
    C. excessive flue gas temperature
    D. low water in boiler

15. A pressuretrol is usually connected directly to the

    A. water side of a boiler
    B. flue gas side of a boiler
    C. steam side of a boiler
    D. discharge side of fuel line

16. A modutrol motor on a typical automatic oil burner firing #6 oil may be used to directly control the

    A. speed of the oil pump or vaporstat
    B. primary air, secondary air, and oil control valve
    C. 3-way magnetic oil valve and magnetic gas valve
    D. electric fuel oil preheater and aquastat

Questions 17-20.

DIRECTIONS: Questions 17 to 20 inclusive are to be answered by referring to the drawing symbols of screwed fittings and valves shown below.

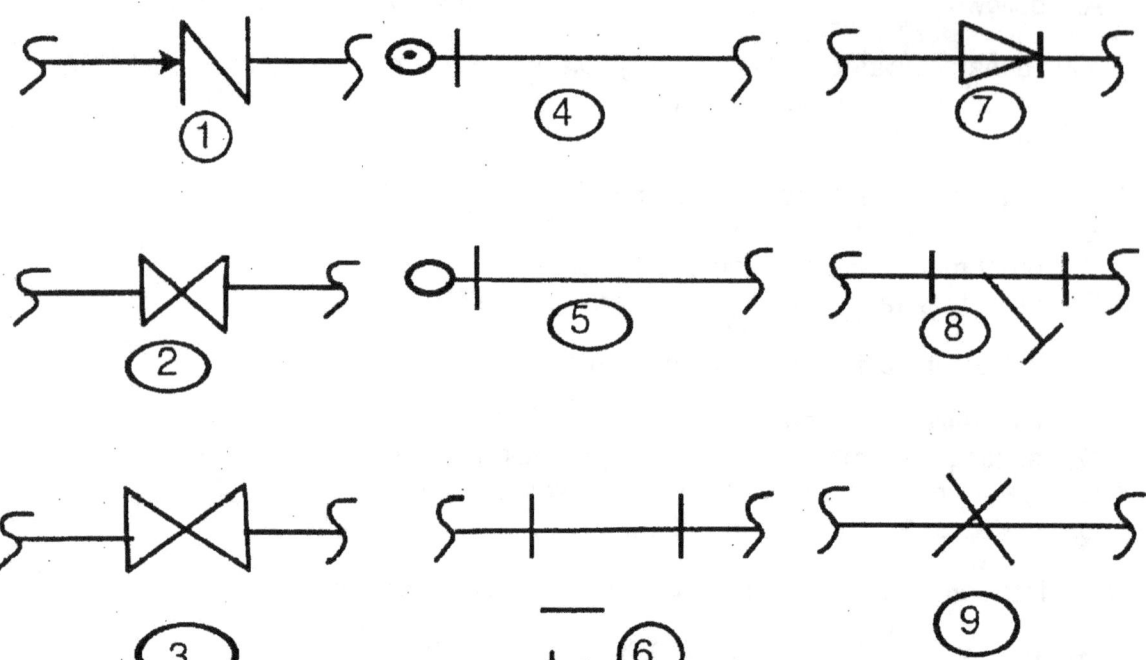

17. Referring to the above sketches, the one representing a turned-up elbow is numbered

    A. 4   B. 5   C. 6   D. 8

18. Referring to the above sketches, the one representing a check valve is numbered

    A. 1   B. 3   C. 7   D. 9

19. Referring to the above sketches, the one representing a globe valve is numbered

    A. 9   B. 3   C. 2   D. 1

20. Referring to the above sketches, the one representing a strainer is numbered

    A. 3   B. 7   C. 9   D. 8

21. The minimum size of pipe that should be used to connect a water column to a low pressure steam boiler is *most nearly*

    A. 3/8"   B. 1/2"   C. 3/4"   D. 1"

22. Of the following metals, the one which is classified as a ferrous metal is

    A. lead   B. iron   C. tin   D. zinc

23. Of the following types of pipe, the one which will expand the MOST when heated is

    A. copper   B. wrought iron
    C. steel   D. brass

24. Of the following devices, the ones that are usually used to provide for expansion in a long horizontal run of hot water pipe are   24._____

   A. clamps B. anchors
   C. swivel offsets D. pipe stanchions

25. The MINIMUM diameter of pipe that may be used for gas piping is   25._____

   A. 3/4" B. 5/8" C. 1/2" D. 3/8"

26. The type of thread that is used on standard iron pipe size brass pipe is known as the   26._____

   A. Witworth Standard B. Briggs Standard
   C. British Association D. Standard Acme

27. The taper on a standard pipe thread is *most nearly* _____ to the foot.   27._____

   A. 1/8" B. 1/4" C. 1/2" D. 3/4"

28. Of the following statements concerning the use of lamp wick on screwed pipe joints, the one which is *most nearly* CORRECT is that   28._____

   A. it may suggest the existence of imperfect threads
   B. it is the best modern day practice
   C. the joints are strengthened
   D. pipe compound is not needed

29. Of the following wrenches, the one which is used MOST often for making up connections to a boiler is the _____ wrench.   29._____

   A. monkey B. open end C. strap D. pipe

30. Boiler fusible plugs are usually filled with   30._____

   A. lead B. copper C. tin D. solder

31. The capacity, in gallons, of a 10'-0" diameter by 21'-0" high cylindrical tank with flat heads is *most nearly*   31._____

   A. 1650 B. 2100 C. 6900 D. 12,500

32. "The water level in the gage glass was *dormant* during the peak load conditions." As used in this sentence, the word *dormant* means *most nearly*   32._____

   A. fluctuating B. inactive
   C. clean D. foaming

33. The instructor's words were understood but *irrelevant*. As used in this sentence, the word *irrelevant* means *most nearly*   33._____

   A. unchallenging to the audience
   B. unconvincing to the audience
   C. not bearing upon the subject under discussion
   D. not based upon facts

34. The MOST important requirement of a good inspectional report is that it should be   34._____

   A. properly addressed B. lengthy
   C. clear and brief D. spelled correctly

35. Building superintendents frequently inquire about departmental inspectional procedures. Of the following, it is BEST to

    A. advise them to write to the department for an official reply
    B. refuse as the inspectional procedure is a restricted matter
    C. briefly explain the procedure to them
    D. avoid the inquiry by changing the subject

36. In making an inspection of a boiler repair job in progress in a private building, an inspector's PRIMARY concern should be to

    A. avoid conversation with the building superintendent
    B. concentrate on the workmanship of the men
    C. anticipate construction problems before they occur
    D. ascertain whether or not the repair job is in accordance with the code and regulations of the department

Questions 37-40.

DIRECTIONS: Questions 37 to 40, inclusive, are to be answered in accordance with the following paragraph.

A low pressure hot water boiler shall include a relief valve or valves of a capacity such that with the heat generating equipment operating at maximum, the pressure cannot rise more than 20 percent above the maximum allowable working pressure (set pressure) if that is 30 p.s.i. gage or less, nor more than 10 percent if it is more than 30 p.s.i. gage. The difference between the set pressure and the pressure at which the valve is relieving is known as "overpressure or accumulation." If the steam relieving capacity in pounds per hour is calculated, it shall be determined by dividing by 1,000 the maximum Btu output at the boiler nozzle obtainable from the heat generating equipment, or by multiplying the square feet of heating surface by five.

37. In accordance with the above paragraph, the capacity of a relief valve should be computed on the basis of

    A. size of boiler
    B. maximum rated capacity of generating equipment
    C. average output of the generating equipment
    D. minimum capacity of generating equipment

38. In accordance with the above paragraph, with a set pressure of 30 p.s.i. gage, the overpressure should NOT be more than _____ p.s.i.

    A. 3   B. 6   C. 33   D. 36

39. In accordance with the above paragraph, a relief valve should start relieving at a pressure equal to the _____ pressure.

    A. set
    B. over
    C. overpressure minus set
    D. set pressure plus over

40. In accordance with the above paragraph, the steam relieving capacity can be computed by

   A. multiplying the maximum BTU output by 5
   B. dividing the pounds of steam per hour by 1000
   C. dividing the maximum BTU output by the square feet of heating surface
   D. dividing the maximum BTU output by 1000

40._____

KEY (CORRECT ANSWERS)

1.	A	11.	A	21.	D	31.	D
2.	B	12.	B	22.	B	32.	B
3.	B	13.	C	23.	A	33.	C
4.	D	14.	A	24.	C	34.	C
5.	A	15.	C	25.	D	35.	C
6.	D	16.	B	26.	B	36.	D
7.	B	17.	A	27.	D	37.	B
8.	B	18.	A	28.	A	38.	B
9.	C	19.	B	29.	D	39.	D
10.	C	20.	D	30.	C	40.	D

EXAMINATION SECTION
TEST 1

DIRECTIONS: Each question or incomplete statement is followed by several suggested answers or completions. Select the one that BEST answers the question or completes the statement. *PRINT THE LETTER OF THE CORRECT ANSWER IN THE SPACE AT THE RIGHT.*

1. A boiler horsepower is NOT defined as

   A. the evaporation of 34.5 lbs. of water per hour
   B. 33,475 Btu's
   C. 12 square feet of heating surface
   D. 12,000 Btu's per hour

2. The MOST important valve on a boiler is the _____ valve.

   A. stop-check   B. blow-down
   C. safety   D. vacuum breaker

3. A fusible plug is a plug that is

   A. installed on boilers to protect the boiler from dangerously low water
   B. inserted into a leaky tube
   C. installed on a pipe after the pipe has been disconnected from the boiler
   D. none of the above

4. A fusible plug is constructed of

   A. solid brass   B. bronze *only*
   C. bronze and tin   D. stainless steel

5. The melting point of a fusible plug is _____ degrees F.

   A. 450   B. 375   C. 200   D. 100

6. The pressure limitation for a fusible plug is _____ psi.

   A. 175   B. 225   C. 250   D. 300

7. The fusible plugs in a boiler are NOT placed in

   A. the crown sheet of a locomotive boiler
   B. one of the tubes of a vertical boiler
   C. the tube sheet of an H.R.T. boiler
   D. the drum of a water tube boiler

8. The valve NOT necessary on a boiler is the

   A. safety   B. stop-check
   C. blow-down   D. angle

9. If a boiler generates 4,000 lbs. of steam per hour, _____ Safety valves are required

   A. 1   B. 2   C. 3   D. 4

10. A low-water cut-off

    A. cuts off all water to the boiler
    B. cuts off the water on a blow-off
    C. shuts off the fuel supply to the boiler in the event of low water in the boiler
    D. keeps the water level up

11. The purpose of a stop-check valve is to

    A. stop the flow of steam when there is no demand
    B. prevent the backflow of steam into the boiler in the event of boiler failure
    C. stop the condensate from entering the boiler
    D. inject steam into the lines

12. The purpose of a blow-off valve is to blow off

    A. excess steam
    B. soot from the boiler
    C. impurities from the lowest point of the boiler
    D. excess condensate entering the boiler

13. A *pig-tail* is installed on a steam line to

    A. prevent air from getting into the steam lines
    B. create a vacuum in the line
    C. put the gauge up higher so it may be visible to the engineer
    D. prevent live steam from damaging the steam gauge

14. A steam injector is used on a steam boiler to

    A. heat the oil before it enters the boiler
    B. inject steam into the line for velocity
    C. force water into the boiler
    D. inject air into the boiler

15. Two hydrometer gas valves are installed on a gas main

    A. to insure efficiency
    B. to increase the gas pressure
    C. so that if one valve fails to open, the other valve will open
    D. so that if one valve fails to open, the other valve will not open

16. The bottom blow-off on a water tube boiler is located

    A. just below the section drum
    B. in between the two upper drums
    C. under the boiler
    D. at the rear of the boiler on the mud drum

17. The dry pipe on a boiler is located

    A. just below the last row of tubes
    B. below the superheater
    C. at the top of the steam and water drum
    D. between the superheater and the engine

18. The purpose of a superheater is to	18._____

    A. remove excess moisture from the steam
    B. create dry steam
    C. permit the engine to run more efficiently with superheated steam
    D. all of the above

19. Water wall tubes are used	19._____

    A. to insure proper amounts of water to the boiler
    B. because the boiler must have a certain number of tubes per boiler horsepower
    C. to carry off the excess heat from the furnace walls
    D. to create more steam

20. At what degree are the readings on the Celsius and Fahrenheit scale the same?	20._____

    A. 100   B. 212
    C. 10 below zero   D. 40 below zero

21. At what temperature does water boil on the celsius scale? _____ degrees.	21._____

    A. 100   B. 175   C. 212   D. 273

22. *Sensible heat* is the	22._____

    A. quality of heat required to change the state or condition without a change in temperature
    B. heat which produces an increase in temperature, as distinguished from latent heat, which produces a change in state
    C. heat indicating how hot or cold a substance is
    D. none of these

23. All of the following are functions of a separator EXCEPT: To	23._____

    A. increase the quality of steam
    B. extract condensate from the steam
    C. extract any oil or impurities from the steam
    D. equalize the steam pressure

24. The instrument used to record air-flow to steam-flow relationship is a	24._____

    A. hydrometer   B. steam flow meter
    C. pryometer   D. velocity meter

25. The gasket suitable for a flange on an oil line operating at 300 degrees F. is a(n) _____ gasket.	25._____

    A. rubber   B. asbestos
    C. oil paper   D. metallic

26. You would NOT install a valve marked 300 W.O.G. on a(n) _____ line carrying 250 psi.	26._____

    A. steam   B. water   C. gas   D. oil

27. A cause of high stack temperature is

   A. poor combustion
   B. sooty or scaled tubes
   C. poor water circulation
   D. none of these

28. The purpose of a barometric damper is to

   A. *increase* the draft pressure in the boiler
   B. *increase* the CO_2, and *decrease* the CO
   C. *decrease* the CO_2, and *increase* the CO
   D. *decrease* the CO_2 at the boiler outlet

29. API degree refers to the

   A. stamping on the boiler plate
   B. viscosity of oil
   C. temperature of oil
   D. American Petroleum Institute

30. If a boiler has 1,000 square feet of heating surface, what would the boiler horsepower be, assuming 12 square feet per BHP?

   A. 83.3   B. 1,012   C. 1,200   D. 12,000

KEY (CORRECT ANSWERS)

1.	D	16.	D
2.	C	17.	C
3.	A	18.	D
4.	C	19.	C
5.	A	20.	D
6.	C	21.	A
7.	D	22.	B
8.	D	23.	D
9.	B	24.	B
10.	C	25.	B
11.	B	26.	A
12.	C	27.	D
13.	D	28.	D
14.	C	29.	B
15.	D	30.	A

TEST 2

DIRECTIONS: Each question or incomplete statement is followed by several suggested answers or completions. Select the one that BEST answers the question or completes the statement. *PRINT THE LETTER OF THE CORRECT ANSWER IN THE SPACE AT THE RIGHT.*

1. In setting the nozzle pressure on a boiler WITHOUT a manometer, in order to obtain the inches of water column you should take the ounces of gas pressure and multiply by 1.____

   A. 0.5781 B. 1.73 C. 3.1416 D. 33,475

2. How many safety valves are required on a boiler having at LEAST 500 square feet? 2.____

   A. 1 B. 2 C. 3 D. 4

3. The FIRST thing to do before attempting to make a *major* repair to a boiler is to 3.____

   A. check to see if there is a qualified person who can do the repairs
   B. make sure parts are available for the repairs
   C. notify the insurance carrier to send an inspector who will recommend how the repairs should be done
   D. notify the insurance company to recommend a company to do the repairs

4. Which of the following methods is NOT employed with domestic hot water systems? 4.____

   A. Upfeed risers with returns having no connections paralleling the risers
   B. One main upfeed riser without connections, supplying all down feed risers for all fixtures
   C. Upfeed risers without connections, supplying a down feed riser for all fixtures
   D. Upfeed risers with returns in other locations, with connections taken off both supply and return

5. A steam gauge should be connected to a high pressure steam line with a(n) 5.____

   A. coupling B. syphon
   C. union D. ell and coupling

6. Coal is composed of 6.____

   A. moisture B. fixed ash or carbon
   C. volatile matters D. all of the above

7. If absolute pressure is 215 psia, what is the equivalent gauge pressure in psig? 7.____

   A. 190 B. 195 C. 200 D. 205

8. The valve between the fuel oil heater and the burner valve is called the _____ valve. 8.____

   A. check B. safety C. root D. stop

9. The purpose of a tube retarder is to 9.____

   A. help circulate the water around the tubes
   B. prevent sagging of the tubes
   C. slow down the water circulation around the tubes
   D. restrict the combustible gases from traveling at a great speed through the tubes, giving more heat on the water side of the boiler

31

10. On a Scotch Marine boiler, the sheets on the side of the combustion chamber are called _____ sheets.

    A. crown
    B. wrapper
    C. bridge wall
    D. dry

11. The *primary* purpose of a steam injector is to pump water into the

    A. boiler while being tested
    B. boiler after the main feed pump fails to operate
    C. main condenser
    D. none of these

12. The *proper* way to blow down the bottom blow-off is by

    A. letting the water level drop slightly
    B. increasing the steam pressure
    C. adding about 2" of water to the boiler above the normal level
    D. increasing the oil pressure

13. If oil or scale is present on boiler tubes, the result will be

    A. oxidation
    B. overheating
    C. galvanic action
    D. over-lubrication

14. To maintain the proper water level on a manually-controlled feedwater system, you should

    A. operate the feed-check valve
    B. open the recirculating valve
    C. start the secondary feed pump
    D. open the feed pump stem valve

15. If the water in the sight glass is empty, you should

    A. add another feed pump on the line
    B. replace the check valve
    C. secure all burners
    D. close the feed stop valve

16. On a water tube boiler, the internal feed line is located at the

    A. top of the bottom drum
    B. top of the furnace
    C. bottom of the steam and water drum
    D. top of the steam and water drum

17. It is legal to install a *Y* branch fitting on a boiler

    A. on the water and steam drum
    B. in the combustion chamber
    C. on the wrapper sheet
    D. on the feedwater circulating pump

18. The purpose of a surface blow-down valve is to   18._____

    A. remove sludge and scale from the boiler
    B. blow down excess water if the level is too high
    C. remove all oil and scum from the surface
    D. help drain the boiler

19. A main condenser is used to   19._____

    A. convert steam into water
    B. convert water into steam
    C. increase the back pressure for better efficiency
    D. remove all air from the air chamber

20. If the condenser vacuum feed valve were left open, it would result in   20._____

    A. loss of condensate water
    B. vacuum loss
    C. intermittent loss of vacuum
    D. all of the above

21. A safety valve should be installed   21._____

    A. with a union
    B. with a coupling
    C. on top of a gate valve
    D. on the boiler without any other valve between the safety valve and the boiler

22. A stop or non-return valve   22._____

    A. is a valve attached to the steam outlet of a boiler which will close automatically if there is a pressure part failure in the boiler
    B. is used to prevent backflow of steam from the steam header to the point of failure
    C. will isolate automatically a defective boiler supplying steam to the same header
    D. all of the above

23. A blow-off valve is used to   23._____

    A. discharge mud from the boiler
    B. discharge all scale and impurities from the boiler
    C. lower high water level
    D. all of the above

24. A *pop* or blow back ring is   24._____

    A. located on a blow-down valve
    B. located on a non-return valve
    C. located on an orsat device
    D. used to regulate the blow down or closing pressure of a safety valve

25. The blow back ring affects the opening pressure of a safety valve by

    A. increasing the back pressure
    B. relieving the counter balance of any pressure
    C. affecting the closing pressure only, NOT the opening pressure
    D. helping to relieve the pressure quickly

26. The MOST common breakdowns in a boiler are in

    A. bulges in the shell
    B. leaky or split tubes
    C. faulty staybolts
    D. all of the above

27. Cracks *normally* occur

    A. around the rivet holes
    B. at flanged corners
    C. between tube openings
    D. all of the above

28. Repairs of cracks should be made by

    A. cutting the crack a little bigger, then welding it
    B. drilling small holes in each corner of the crack, preventing further extension, then patching over the crack
    C. cutting out a section in the shape of a square, then welding a patch either inside or outside
    D. none of the above

29. A hydrokineter is a(n)

    A. nozzle located inside a scotch marine boiler which helps circulate cool water while steam is blowing through the nozzle
    B. nozzle on the bottom of a scotch marine boiler to extract boiler water for testing
    C. instrument used with a salinity indicator
    D. instrument for measuring high temperatures

30. A manometer is an instrument used to measure

    A. draft and pressure by inches of water column
    B. air pressure
    C. amount of fuel
    D. the heating surface of a boiler

KEY (CORRECT ANSWERS)

1.	B	16.	C
2.	B	17.	A
3.	C	18.	C
4.	C	19.	A
5.	B	20.	C
6.	D	21.	D
7.	C	22.	D
8.	C	23.	D
9.	D	24.	D
10.	B	25.	C
11.	B	26.	D
12.	C	27.	D
13.	B	28.	B
14.	A	29.	A
15.	C	30.	A

TEST 3

DIRECTIONS: Each question or incomplete statement is followed by several suggested answers or completions. Select the one that BEST answers the question or completes the statement. *PRINT THE LETTER OF THE CORRECT ANSWER IN THE SPACE AT THE RIGHT.*

1. The MINIMUM size of pipe used on a blow-down connection on a high pressure boiler is   1.___

   A. 1½" B. 1 3/4" C. 2" D. 2½"

2. To convert cubic feet into pounds, multiply by   2.___

   A. 2.31 B. 1,728 C. 62.4 D. 144

3. Pressure is measured in   3.___

   A. cubic feet
   C. pounds per square feet
   B. pounds per square inch
   D. foot pounds

4. Pressure at sea level is _____ psi.   4.___

   A. 14.7 B. 15 C. 19 D. 25

5. Atmospheric pressure affects the operation of a steam engine by   5.___

   A. increasing the compression
   B. reducing the power and acting as a back pressure on the engine piston
   C. keeping the governor from lifting
   D. cutting back the exhaust

6. Atmospheric pressure can be relieved by   6.___

   A. using a back pressure valve
   B. using a condenser
   C. cutting back the pressure
   D. exhausting some of the pressure to the atmosphere

7. Atmospheric pressure is measured with a   7.___

   A. manometer
   C. barometer
   B. pyrometer
   D. hydrometer

8. The pressure of a low-pressure system is _____ psi.   8.___

   A. 10 B. 15 C. 25 D. 50

9. _____ draft is CORRECT for a boiler.   9.___

   A. Natural
   C. Induced
   B. Forced
   D. All of the above

10. Which of the following stays are IMPORTANT in the construction of a boiler?   10.___

    A. Gusset
    C. Diagonal
    B. Rivet
    D. All of the above

36

11. A ligament is the 11.____

   A. weld between two plates
   B. metal between a butt joint
   C. segment of tube sheet between the tubes
   D. metal between the back pitch

12. Water is cooled in a cooling tower by 12.____

   A. radiation   B. convection
   C. evaporation   D. all of the above

13. At LEAST _____ sq. ft. is needed to cool water in a cooling tower. 13.____

   A. 100   B. 175   C. 250   D. 1,000

14. A cooling tower is used to cool 14.____

   A. boiler condensate and extract impurities
   B. water for air conditioning
   C. water that is being returned to a boiler
   D. none of the above

15. To set the pressure on a safety valve use 15.____

   A. the hydrostatic method
   B. the gauge pressure on the boiler
   C. pneumatic pressure
   D. none of the above

16. If the pressure setting on a safety valve attached to a superheater is set to relieve at 200 16.____
    psig, what should the pressure setting of the boiler safety valve be, in psig?

   A. 195   B. 200   C. 205   D. 225

17. There is sufficient amount of water in a boiler when 17.____

   A. the water in the gauge glass is filled to the top
   B. water starts to run out of the safety valve
   C. all the surface exposed to intense heat is submerged
   D. the boiler is half filled with water

18. To determine whether the boiler has the CORRECT level of water 18.____

   A. open the blow down valve, then check the water glass
   B. fill the boiler until the water glass is filled
   C. close the drain cock on the water glass until all the water has disappeared
   D. blow down the low water cut-off, then check the water glass for the true level

19. How much water should be carried in a vertical boiler? 19.____

   A. Half the boiler should be filled with water
   B. The water level should be 3" above the top row of tubes
   C. The water should be as high as possible without causing wet stream
   D. The water level should be about two thirds filled

20. The advantage of high water level in a vertical boiler is that it

   A. increases the efficiency of the tubular heating surface
   B. increases the steam space of the boiler
   C. produces superheated steam
   D. none of the above

21. A compound gauge measures

   A. ounces and water pressure
   B. vacuum and atmospheric pressure
   C. pressure and vacuum
   D. vacuum and absolute pressure

22. A steam gauge functions by

   A. steam pressure raising the gauge to the desired reading
   B. the expansion of a corrugated diaphragm when pressure is applied
   C. water and steam pressure combining to raise the pressure on the gauge
   D. none of the above

23. A water column

   A. indicates the pressure at the base
   B. contains a float which actuates a whistle when the water level drops below a safe level
   C. is installed on a condensate pump to indicate the amount of water in the receiver tank
   D. is a water gauge on a feedwater tank

24. How many gallons are there in an oil tank 10 feet high and 3 feet in diameter?

   A. 528.7   B. 5,089   C. 55,000   D. 508,940

25. What is the pressure in lbs., on the bottom of a feed-water tank filled with water, if it is 14 ft. long and 28 in. in diamerer?

   A. 3,600   B. 3,731   C. 4,275   D. 5,125

26. How many gallons are there in a tank 10 feet in diameter and 23 feet long?

   A. 11,700   B. 13,600   C. 15,800   D. none of these

27. What is the pressure in lbs., on the bottom of the tank in the preceding question?

   A. 95,000   B. 110,600   C. 112,563   D. 135,862

28. A city of 30,000 people consumes 1,500 gallons of water per minute from a holding tank of 250,000 gallons that is 200 feet high.
   What horsepower motor is required to replace this water, using the formula:

   $$HP = \frac{FOOT - POUNDS}{33,000 \, xt} \, ?$$

   A. 75 HP   B. 113 HP   C. 126 HP   D. 151 HP

29. To convert gallons of water to cubic feet, multiply by
    A. .1337　　B. 3.785　　C. 128　　D. 231

30. The MAXIMUM theoretical lift of water at sea level is _____ feet.
    A. 12　　B. 28　　C. 34　　D. 50

KEY (CORRECT ANSWERS)

1. A
2. C
3. B
4. A
5. B

6. B
7. C
8. B
9. D
10. D

11. C
12. D
13. C
14. B
15. D

16. C
17. C
18. D
19. C
20. A

21. C
22. B
23. B
24. A
25. B

26. D
27. C
28. C
29. A
30. C

EXAMINATION SECTION
TEST 1

DIRECTIONS: Each question or incomplete statement is followed by several suggested answers or completions. Select the one that BEST answers the question or completes the statement. *PRINT THE LETTER OF THE CORRECT ANSWER IN THE SPACE AT THE RIGHT.*

1. An *unloader* is a device that is commonly found on a(n)
   A. steam header
   B. air compressor
   C. anemometer
   D. soot blower

2. An instrument for drawing a diagram showing actual pressure-volume relationships within the cylinder of an engine or a compressor is called a(n)
   A. barometer
   B. engine indicator
   C. pyrometer
   D. venturi meter

3. Air compressor suction and discharge valves should be cleaned with
   A. naphtha   B. benzene   C. fuel oil   D. soap suds

4. Of the following valves, the BEST one to use to restrict or throttle a flow of fluid is a _____ valve.
   A. gate
   B. quick-opening
   C. globe
   D. plug

5. The MAIN reason that try-cocks are installed on a boiler is to ensure that the
   A. boiler can be blown down
   B. water column can be blown down
   C. water gage glass is operating correctly
   D. condensate pumps are operating

6. A direct-acting duplex reciprocating steam pump is designated as 6 x 3 x 7. The numeral 6 indicates the
   A. diameter of the water cylinders
   B. length of stroke of both cylinders
   C. diameter of the steam cylinders
   D. diameter of the admission valve

7. The one of the following pumps that has NO moving parts is the _____ pump.
   A. plunger
   B. jet
   C. radial flow
   D. piston

8. Of the following types of pumps, the one which is MOST generally used to pump fuel oil is the _____ type pump.
   A. jet
   B. rotary
   C. centrifugal
   D. propeller

9. The test pressure recommended for a hydrostatic test of a boiler is _____ the working pressure.

    A. 2 1/2 times   B. 2 times   C. 1 1/2 times   D. equal to

10. Assume that a boiler has been out of service for repairs and is now ready to be put back on the line.
Of the following, the FIRST step operating personnel should take is to

    A. fill the boiler with water
    B. open the vents
    C. blow boiler tubes
    D. inspect the inside and outside of the boiler

11. The one of the following that is a water-tube boiler is the _____ boiler.

    A. horizontal return tubular
    B. bent-tube
    C. economic
    D. horizontal two-pass

12. An oil-fired high pressure boiler has to be taken off the line.
Of the following procedures, the FIRST step would be to

    A. reduce the fuel feed and slowly decrease the output
    B. manually close the non-return valve
    C. open the drain connections between the non-return and the head stop valve
    D. close the feedwater-supply valve

13. A drop in steam pressure, as indicated by the steam gauge, of a normally operating steam boiler would MOST likely indicate that the

    A. fuel supply must be increased
    B. boiler must be blown down
    C. speed of the feedwater pump must be increased
    D. low water cut-off is inoperative

14. Steam that has been heated above the temperature corresponding to its pressure is said to be

    A. superheated   B. pressurized
    C. tempered   D. overheated

15. In a shutdown of a boiler to prevent the creation of a vacuum from the condensing steam within the boiler, the steam drum vent valve should be opened when the steam pressure has dropped to approximately _____ psi.

    A. 100   B. 75   C. 50   D. 25

16. An attemperator is a device used to control or regulate

    A. air temperature   B. steam temperature
    C. oil pressure   D. water pressure

17. The number of safety valves on the boiler drum of a power boiler with a heating surface of 500 square feet is AT LEAST

    A. 2 B. 3 C. 4 D. 5

18. The fusible plug of an HRT boiler is located in the

    A. hot water tank
    B. rear head
    C. fire door
    D. water column

19. Boiler tube size is designated by its

    A. boiler location
    B. wall thickness
    C. external diameter
    D. internal diameter

20. A feedwater heater is installed in a steam generating system PRIMARILY to

    A. furnish hot water to the building
    B. generate hot feedwater for the building radiators
    C. condition and heat feedwater to the boiler
    D. distribute high pressure steam

KEY (CORRECT ANSWERS)

1.	B	11.	B
2.	B	12.	A
3.	D	13.	A
4.	C	14.	A
5.	C	15.	D
6.	C	16.	B
7.	B	17.	A
8.	B	18.	B
9.	C	19.	C
10.	D	20.	C

TEST 2

DIRECTIONS: Each question or incomplete statement is followed by several suggested answers or completions. Select the one that BEST answers the question or completes the statement. *PRINT THE LETTER OF THE CORRECT ANSWER IN THE SPACE AT THE RIGHT.*

1. A balanced draft in a boiler consists of

    A. a forced draft fan only
    B. a natural chimney draft only
    C. both forced and induced draft
    D. both induced and natural draft

    1.____

2. One horsepower is *electrically equivalent* to 746

    A. watts   B. calories   C. joules   D. kilowatts

    2.____

3. Of the following pH values, the one which indicates that a solution is *neither* acid *nor* alkaline is

    A. 3   B. 4   C. 7   D. 10

    3.____

4. Zinc bars are sometimes placed in boilers to

    A. increase the pH value of the feedwater
    B. eliminate foul gases in the steam
    C. prevent corrosion
    D. decrease foaming and priming

    4.____

5. The MAIN function of an evaporator is to remove impurities in

    A. air   B. oil   C. water   D. grease

    5.____

6. The MAIN reason why a caustic boil-out of a boiler would be necessary is that the boiler has accumulated a deposit of

    A. sediment   B. oil   C. scale   D. slime

    6.____

7. Of the following, the type of steam traps that does NOT have any moving parts is the

    A. inverted bucket   B. impulse
    C. continuous-flow   D. float-actuated

    7.____

8. The one of the following valves that permits fluid to flow in one direction only is the

    A. check   B. plug   C. globe   D. stop

    8.____

9. A 1/2 inch diameter galvanized pipe that is 3" long and has male threads at both ends is known as a

    A. tube   B. flange   C. joint   D. nipple

    9.____

10. The one of the following pipe fittings that should be used to connect a 1 1/2"-diameter pipe is a(n)

    A. saddle   B. increaser   C. elbow   D. nipple

    10.____

44

11. A receiver in a compressed air system 11.____

    A. stores lubricating oil
    B. stores compressed air
    C. furnishes air to the air compressor
    D. acts as a pressure relief

12. The device that stops or starts a fully automatic oil burner at a predetermined pressure is 12.____
    called a

    A. hydrostat   B. thermostat
    C. pressuretrol   D. transformer

13. Of the following statements, the one which is CORRECT as pertains to a closed-type 13.____
    feedwater heater is that the

    A. steam and water mix
    B. water will be heated to within a few degrees of the steam temperature
    C. feedwater heater is located at an elevation above the boiler feed pump
    D. floating impurities are removed from the surface of the water through the overflow
       weir

14. The function of *cooling towers* is to 14.____

    A. cool condenser water
    B. supply drinking water
    C. cool the boiler room
    D. circulate the boiler feedwater

15. The function of an oil separator in a non-condensing steam plant is to remove oil from 15.____

    A. exhaust steam   B. compressed air
    C. feedwater   D. liquid ammonia

16. An economizer is generally located between the 16.____

    A. feedwater heater and feed pump
    B. air compressor and receiver
    C. suction and discharge oil strainers
    D. boiler and the stack

17. Of the following types of equipment used to remove fly ash from flue gases, the one 17.____
    which is the MOST commonly installed in commercial boilers is the

    A. electrostatic precipitator
    B. mechanical collector
    C. fabric filter
    D. wet scrubber

18. The one of the following general classes of stokers in which coal is admitted below the 18.____
    point of air admission is the _____ stoker.

    A. underfeed   B. chain grate
    C. traveling grate   D. spreader

19. The fuel bed of an underfeed stoker has the green coal at the 19.____

    A. bottom
    B. top
    C. middle
    D. burning surface

20. The one of the following coals that has a restriction on its use in New York City is 20.____

    A. canel
    B. lignite
    C. bituminous
    D. anthracite

KEY (CORRECT ANSWERS)

1.	C	11.	B
2.	A	12.	C
3.	C	13.	B
4.	C	14.	A
5.	C	15.	A
6.	B	16.	D
7.	C	17.	A
8.	A	18.	A
9.	D	19.	A
10.	B	20.	C

EXAMINATION SECTION
TEST 1

DIRECTIONS: Each question or incomplete statement is followed by several suggested answers or completions. Select the one that BEST answers the question or completes the statement. *PRINT THE LETTER OF THE CORRECT ANSWER IN THE SPACE AT THE RIGHT.*

1. The method used in a hand-fired furnace wherein the coal is fired on one side of the furnace while the other side is burning brightly is known as the _____ method.   1._____

    A. coking   B. spreading   C. ribbon   D. alternate

2. The measure of a fluid's resistance to flow is known as   2._____

    A. viscosity   B. hydrodynamics
    C. continuity   D. polarity

3. Demulsibility is the ability of a lubricating oil to separate from   3._____

    A. air   B. steam   C. flue gas   D. water

4. The wick in a gravity oil-feed system is generally made of   4._____

    A. rayon   B. wool   C. cotton   D. nylon

5. The temperature range to which No. 6 low sulphur fuel oil must *normally* be heated for proper atomization is _____ °F.   5._____

    A. 220-240   B. 170-200   C. 140-160   D. 120-130

6. When fuel oil is dispersed from an oil burner as a fine mist, it is said to be   6._____

    A. impelled   B. atomized
    C. crystallized   D. filtered

7. The one of the following devices that controls the fuel oil temperature leaving the oil heater is a (n)   7._____

    A. interlock   B. aquastat
    C. modutrol   D. accumulator

8. A duplex oil strainer is installed in a fuel oil line to   8._____

    A. remove impurities at twice the rate of oil flow
    B. change the direction of flow of the oil
    C. facilitate the use of various grades of oil
    D. allow uninterrupted flow of oil when one strainer is removed and cleaned

9. The oil burner *remote control switch* should generally be located   9._____

    A. on the oil burner housing
    B. at the entrance to the boiler room
    C. on a wall nearest the oil transfer pump
    D. on top of the boiler drum

10. The control that starts and stops the flow of oil to the spinning cup of a rotary cup oil burner is the

    A. magnetic oil valve   B. transformer
    C. electrode   D. bellows

11. Spontaneous combustion ignition is MOST likely to occur in a pile of

    A. loose planks   B. oily tools
    C. oily rags   D. masonite scrapings

12. Electric current is measured in units of

    A. ohms   B. amperes   C. volts   D. farads

13. A circuit breaker serves the same function as a

    A. meter   B. resistor   C. fuse   D. solenoid

14. A lead expansion anchor would normally be used to attach a bracket to a

    A. plaster ceiling   B. masonite wall
    C. brass pipe   D. concrete wall

15. The hardness of water is expressed in units of

    A. gpm   B. ppm   C. cop   D. stp

16. The alkaline contents of boiler feedwater can be *decreased* by

    A. blowing down the boiler
    B. adding caustic soda
    C. increasing the firing rate
    D. decreasing the speed of the feedwater pump

17. The MAJOR cause of air pollution resulting from burning fuel oil is

    A. carbon monoxide   B. sulphur dioxide
    C. nitrogen   D. hydrogen

18. The CO_2 content in the flue gas of an efficiently fired boiler should be approximately

    A. 30%   B. 25%   C. 15%   D. 12%

19. Of the following devices, the one which is used to determine the CO_2 content in flue gases is a(n)

    A. orsat   B. haze gauge
    C. ammeter   D. venturi

20. The one of the following that is known as an *actuating control* is a

    A. bellows   B. heliostat
    C. needle valve   D. relay

KEY (CORRECT ANSWERS)

1.	D	11.	C
2.	A	12.	B
3.	D	13.	C
4.	B	14.	D
5.	B	15.	B
6.	B	16.	A
7.	B	17.	B
8.	D	18.	D
9.	B	19.	A
10.	A	20.	D

TEST 2

DIRECTIONS: Each question or incomplete statement is followed by several suggested answers or completions. Select the one that BEST answers the question or completes the statement. *PRINT THE LETTER OF THE CORRECT ANSWER IN THE SPACE AT THE RIGHT.*

1. The function of a *pyrometer* is to measure

   A. hardness
   B. vibration
   C. polarity
   D. temperature

   1.____

2. A simplex type Bourdon-tube gauge is *ordinarily* used on a steam boiler to indicate

   A. height
   B. flow
   C. temperature
   D. pressure

   2.____

3. A *hydrometer* will measure

   A. specific weight
   B. viscosity
   C. specific gravity
   D. water level

   3.____

4. An instrument that is used to measure gas pressure is a

   A. tachometer
   B. spectrometer
   C. potentiometer
   D. manometer

   4.____

5. The packing that is *generally* used on the cold water end of a centrifugal pump is

   A. brass
   B. rubber
   C. flax
   D. graphited-asbestos

   5.____

6. The one of the following wrenches that would *normally* be used on hexagonally-shaped screwed valves and fittings is the _____ wrench.

   A. open-end
   B. torque
   C. adjustable pipe
   D. hook spanner

   6.____

7. A *hickey* is a device that is used to

   A. hang pipe
   B. lift heavy fittings
   C. dig a trench for a steam line
   D. bend pipe

   7.____

8. A pneumatic tool is *normally* operated by

   A. propane   B. water   C. steam   D. air

   8.____

9. If 50 gallons of fuel oil cost $30.00, then 60 gallons of oil at the same rate will cost

   A. $125.00   B. $90.00   C. $36.00   D. $25.00

   9.____

10. Four oil burners using 50 gallons per hour operating together are to burn 100,000 gallons of No. 6 fuel oil. The number of hours that it would take to burn this quantity of oil is

    A. 500   B. 650   C. 825   D. 1,000

    10.____

50

11. The floor area of a boiler room that is 52 feet long and 31 feet wide is _____ square feet.   11._____

    A. 1,562   B. 1,612   C. 1,721   D. 1,832

12. The sum of 5 1/2, 4, 3 1/4, and 2 1/2 is   12._____

    A. 15 1/4   B. 13 1/2   C. 12   D. 10 1/4

13. Most explosions in furnaces with oil-fired units result from *failure* to detect a   13._____

    A. dropping boiler pressure
    B. dropping steam temperature
    C. pulsating exit gas temperature
    D. loss of ignition

14. The MAIN reason why tools should NOT be left on catwalks or scaffolds is to   14._____

    A. prevent a mix-up of tools
    B. prevent the tools from being borrowed
    C. prevent damage to tools if they fell off onto the landing
    D. avoid a safety hazard

15. The proper extinguishing agent to use on a live electrical fire is   15._____

    A. carbon dioxide   B. steam
    C. water   D. foam

16. The FIRST procedure to follow upon witnessing smoke coming from an electronic control unit is to   16._____

    A. call the fire department
    B. pour water on it
    C. shut off the power
    D. look for a fire extinguisher

Questions 17-20.

DIRECTIONS: Questions 17 through 20 are to be answered SOLELY in accordance with the information contained in the following paragraph.

    Steel used in boiler construction must be of a higher quality than steel used in general construction. The boiler steel must be capable of sustaining loads at elevated temperatures. Temperature has a more serious effect upon the boiler fabrication than has the pressure. The material for bolts and studs is conditioned by tempering. The tempering temperature is at least 100° F higher than the service operating temperature. All materials used in boiler construction must be creep resistant to minimize the relaxation in service. Fire box quality plate is used for any part of a boiler exposed to the fire or products of combustion. For parts oi the boiler subject to pressure and not exposed to fire or products of combustion, flange quality plate is used. A small percentage of molybdenum is added to steel in the manufacture of superheater tubes, piping, and valves to increase the ability of these parts to withstand high temperature.

17. Material for bolts and studs used on boilers is conditioned for service by 17.____

   A. tempering
   B. re-tightening
   C. forging
   D. anodizing

18. The part of a boiler that is exposed to products of combustion is made of 18.____

   A. alloy materials
   B. firebox quality plate
   C. flange quality plate
   D. carbon steel

19. Temperature has a more serious effect upon boiler fabrication than has the 19.____

   A. vibration
   B. steam
   C. relaxation
   D. pressure

20. When comparing steel used in boiler construction to steel used in general construction, it can be said that steel used in boiler construction must be of a 20.____

   A. high-weld strength
   B. low-carbon content
   C. lower quality
   D. higher quality

KEY (CORRECT ANSWERS)

1.	D	11.	B
2.	D	12.	A
3.	C	13.	D
4.	D	14.	D
5.	C	15.	A
6.	A	16.	C
7.	D	17.	A
8.	D	18.	B
9.	C	19.	D
10.	A	20.	D

EXAMINATION SECTION
TEST 1

DIRECTIONS: Each question or incomplete statement is followed by several suggested answers or completions. Select the one that BEST answers the question or completes the statement. *PRINT THE LETTER OF THE CORRECT ANSWER IN THE SPACE AT THE RIGHT.*

1. Of the following, the one that is an *inherent* boiler heat loss is the loss due to

    A. dry chimney gases
    B. excess air
    C. unburned gaseous combustibles
    D. radiation from the furnace setting

2. The one of the following flue gases whose presence indicates that MORE excess air is being supplied to a furnace than is being used is

    A. carbon dioxide B. carbon monoxide
    C. nitrogen D. oxygen

3. A pressure gage on a compressed air tank reads 35.3 psi at 70° F.

    If, due to a fire, the temperature of the air in the tank were to increase to 600° F, the gage reading should be MOST NEARLY _____ psi.

    A. 70 B. 75 C. 80 D. 85

4. Of the following types of flow meters, the one that is MOST accurate is a

    A. concentric orifice B. venturi tube
    C. flow nozzle D. pitot tube

5. A spring pop safety valve on a fired high-pressure boiler fails to pop at its set pressure. Which of the following methods should be used to free the valve before retesting it?

    A. Strike the valve body with a soft lead hammer until it pops
    B. Raise the valve lifting-lever and release it
    C. Reduce the spring compression gradually until the valve opens
    D. Unscrew the valve one-quarter turn to relieve the strain on it

6. A device which retains the desired parts of a steam-and-water mixture while rejecting the undesired parts of the mixture is a

    A. check valve B. calorimeter
    C. stud tube D. steam trap

7. The MAIN advantage of using water-tube boilers in preference to fire-tube boilers in an installation is that water-tube boilers can be

    A. built much larger
    B. equipped with superheaters
    C. stoker-fired
    D. made portable

8. The PRIMARY purpose of using phosphate to treat boiler water is to

   A. precipitate the hardness constituents
   B. scavenge the dissolved oxygen
   C. dissolve the calcium
   D. dissolve the magnesium

9. Assume that the set pressure of a safety valve on a power boiler is 100 psi.
   The MINIMUM pressure at which the safety valve must close after blowing down is _____ psi.

   A. 92   B. 94   C. 96   D. 98

10. A one-pound sample of wet steam at a certain pressure has an enthalpy of 960 BTU. For this same pressure, the Steam Tables list the enthalpy of saturated liquid as 130 and of saturated vapor as 1130 BTU.
    The quality of the sample steam is MOST NEARLY

    A. 75%   B. 85%   C. 90%   D. 95%

11. The type of feedwater heater which uses hot flue gases to heat the feedwater is known as a(n)

    A. economizer   B. direct-contact heater
    C. deaerator   D. surface heater

12. The minimum recommended suction head for a centrifugal pump handling feedwater at 300° F is 155 feet.
    If the vapor pressure corresponding to the water temperature is 135 feet and the losses in the suction piping amount to 5 feet, the pump should be located AT LEAST _____ the lowest level of the water in the heater.

    A. 25 feet below   B. 15 feet below
    C. 15 feet above   D. 25 feet above

13. As compared to a power-driven triplex single-acting pump of the same size and operating at the same speed, a steam-driven duplex double-acting pump will

    A. pump more water per minute
    B. give a more uniform discharge
    C. have a higher first cost
    D. be more economical to operate

14. The MAIN advantage of operating a steam engine or steam turbine *condensing* is that it

    A. increases the mean effective pressure in the prime mover
    B. decreases the condensate temperature
    C. permits the use of exhaust steam to drive auxiliary equipment
    D. eliminates the need for separating non-condensibles from the steam

15. The automatic shut-off valves for a water gage installed on a high-pressure boiler must be _____ check valves.

    A. horizontal swing   B. vertical swing
    C. ball   D. spring-loaded

16. The efficiency of a riveted joint is defined as the ratio of the

    A. plate thickness to the rivet diameter
    B. strength of the riveted joint to the strength of a welded joint
    C. strength of the riveted joint to the strength of the solid plate
    D. number of rivets in the first row of the joint to the total number of rivets on one side of the joint

17. A pump delivers 1500 pounds of water per minute against a total head of 200 feet. The water horsepower of this pump is MOST NEARLY

    A. 10   B. 40   C. 100   D. 600

18. In the most usual type of large capacity oil burner using #6 oil, under *fully automatic* control, the atomization of the oil is produced MAINLY by the

    A. pressure from the pump
    B. pressure from the secondary air fan
    C. oil temperature from the heater
    D. rotation of the burner assembly by the motor

19. Which of the following comes the closest to indicating the number of degree-days in a normal heating season in the city?

    A. 3000   B. 4000   C. 5000   D. 6000

20. In which of the following methods of steam generation would you expect to obtain reasonably continuous values of CO_2 CLOSEST to the perfect CO_2 value?
    Automatic

    A. stoker firing with temperature recorder
    B. stoker firing with *hold fire timer*
    C. oil firing with *stack switch*
    D. oil firing with *haze regulator*

21. The loss of heat in stack gases for heavy fuel oils is HIGHEST when the CO_2 content is _____ and the stack temperature is _____.

    A. 12%; 500°   B. 8%; 600°   C. 6%; 700°   D. 14%; 600°

22. A badly sooted HRT boiler under coal firing will show a _____ than a clean boiler.

    A. *higher* CO_2 value
    B. *lower* CO_2 value
    C. *higher* stack temperature
    D. *lower* draft loss

23. A unit heater condensing 50 lbs. of low pressure steam per hour would be rated MOST NEARLY at _____ square feet E.D.R.

    A. 50   B. 100   C. 150   D. 200

24. Which of the following values MOST NEARLY equals one horsepower?

    A. 550 ft.lbs. per sec.   B. 3300 ft.lbs. per min.
    C. 5500 ft.lbs. per hour   D. 10000 ft.lbs. per min.

25. An indicator card from a steam engine is most useful to the engineer in
- A. determining the boiler pressure
- B. determining the engine speed
- C. adjusting the valve setting
- D. computing the mechanical efficiency

25._____

KEY (CORRECT ANSWERS)

1.	A	11.	A
2.	D	12.	A
3.	D	13.	A
4.	B	14.	A
5.	B	15.	C
6.	D	16.	C
7.	A	17.	A
8.	A	18.	D
9.	C	19.	C
10.	B	20.	D

21.	C
22.	C
23.	D
24.	A
25.	C

TEST 2

DIRECTIONS: Each question or incomplete statement is followed by several suggested answers or completions. Select the one that BEST answers the question or completes the statement. *PRINT THE LETTER OF THE CORRECT ANSWER IN THE SPACE AT THE RIGHT.*

1. A centrifugal water pump is direct-driven by a 25 HP 900 RPM electric motor at rated load.
   In order to double the quantity of water delivered, it would be necessary to substitute a motor rated at _____ HP at _____ RPM.

   A. 40; 1200   B. 50; 1200   C. 100; 1800   D. 200; 1800

2. The angle of advance of the eccentric on a D-slide valve steam engine is equal to

   A. the lead angle minus the lap angle
   B. the lead angle plus the lap angle
   C. 90 degrees minus the lead angle
   D. 90 degrees plus the lead and the lap angle

3. Of the following statements pertaining to a duplex steam-driven water pump, the one which is NOT true is that

   A. the slide valves have a steam and an exhaust lap
   B. there is a pause in the flow of water through the discharge valve at the end of the stroke
   C. the piston stroke can be adjusted
   D. an air chamber may be omitted on small sizes

4. The diagram on which a steam throttling process is indicated by a straight horizontal line is the _____ diagram.

   A. PV
   B. Mollier
   C. Ringelman
   D. temperature-entropy

5. The one of the following devices which is useful in preventing damage to a multi-stage turbine rotor due to unequal thermal expansion or contraction is the

   A. thrust bearing
   B. dummy piston and seal
   C. rupture seal
   D. motor-driven turning gear

6. The purpose of a steam turbine's governing system is to control steam flow through the unit, usually in order to keep some other factor constant.
   When a steam turbine is driving an alternator, the factor which is usually kept constant by the governor's operation is the

   A. inlet steam pressure
   B. exhaust steam pressure
   C. shaft speed
   D. power output

7. The speed regulation of a condensing steam turbine operating at 1800 RPM at no load and 1750 RPM at full load is MOST NEARLY

   A. 1%   B. 3%   C. 5%   D. 7%

8. The one of the following statements which is NOT true of the operation of steam turbines is that they

   A. operate most efficiently at high speed
   B. can be operated condensing or non-condensing
   C. can be used to drive centrifugal water pumps
   D. need high viscosity cylinder oil mixed with the steam supply to operate properly

8.____

9. Of the following, the one which is TRUE regarding backpressure steam turbines is that they

   A. operate on the exhaust steam from higher pressure turbines
   B. operate condensing
   C. exhaust through a very large hood
   D. convert a small part of the available heat in the steam into power

9.____

10. An aftercooler on a reciprocating air compressor is used PRIMARILY to

    A. increase compressor capacity
    B. improve compressor efficiency
    C. condense the moisture in the compressed air
    D. cool the lubricating oil

10.____

11. The one of the following tasks which is an example of preventive maintenance is

    A. replacing a leaking water pipe nipple
    B. cleaning the cup on a rotary cup burner
    C. cleaning a completely clogged oil strainer
    D. replacing a blown fuse

11.____

12. The four MAIN causes of failure of three-phase electric motors are

    A. dirt, friction, moisture, single-phasing
    B. friction, moisture, single-phasing, vibration
    C. dirt, moisture, single-phasing, vibration
    D. dirt, friction, moisture, vibration

12.____

13. Assume that an alternator running at a speed of 1800 RPM generates AC voltage at a frequency of 60 cycles per second (Hertz).
    The number of poles in this alternator is

    A. 2   B. 4   C. 6   D. 8

13.____

14. Assume that on an integrating watt-hour meter with 4 dials, the respective pointers from left to right are between 7 and 8, between 5 and 6, between 0 and 1, and between 3 and 4.
    Under these conditions, the reading is

    A. 8614   B. 7503   C. 3168   D. 3067

14.____

15. Assume that an ammeter is properly connected to a current transformer that has a ratio of 80 to 5. When the ammeter indicates 4.0 amperes, the current in the primary circuit is MOST NEARLY _____ amperes.

    A. 4.0   B. 20.0   C. 64.0   D. 80.0

15.____

16. Assume that two alternators, No. 1 and No. 2, are operating in parallel and that alternator No. 1 is taking a greater share of the load than alternator No. 2.
    Of the following, the PROPER method to reapportion the load between the two alternators is to

    A. speed up No. 2
    B. slow down No. 1
    C. increase the excitation of No. 2
    D. adjust the governors of both prime movers

    16._____

17. Which of the following CORRECTLY describes the flow of electric power in a three-phase alternator?
    The input is _____ and the output is _____.

    A. three-phase AC to the stator; single-phase AC from the rotor
    B. three-phase AC to the rotor; single-phase AC from the stator
    C. DC to the stator; three-phase AC from the rotor
    D. DC to the rotor; three-phase AC from the stator

    17._____

18. When the load on a mechanical stoker fired boiler plant furnishing steam for slide valve engine generators drops by 30%, the

    A. stoker should be shut down
    B. fan should be speeded up and the stoker slowed
    C. stoker should be speeded up and the air supply reduced
    D. stoker speed and air supply should be adjusted by reducing both

    18._____

19. Which of the following statements is MOST NEARLY correct?

    A. All types of mechanical stokers may be used with equal efficiency under all types of boilers.
    B. Most stokers are designed with a weak member.
    C. The best type of stoker to use is not dependent upon the type of fuel available.
    D. The advisability of installing stokers is not dependent upon the load.

    19._____

20. The number and size of safety valves required on a high pressure boiler is dependent upon the

    A. size of the boiler drums
    B. amount of heating surface
    C. number of pounds of fuel burned per square foot of grate per hour
    D. size of the steam main

    20._____

21. In changing over a boiler from high pressure (150 lbs. per square inch) to 10 lbs. per square inch, it is USUALLY necessary to

    A. *increase* the size of the safety valves
    B. *decrease* the grate area
    C. *increase* the size of the feedwater piping
    D. *increase* the size of the blow down piping

    21._____

22. A boiler feed injector becomes temporarily steam bound. To correct this condition, the MOST proper action to take is to

    A. increase boiler pressure
    B. reduce suction lift
    C. wrap it with cold rags
    D. bank fire

23. If in your plant the volume of air in cu.ft. per min. for combustion is represented by X, which of the following lowing values of X would MOST NEARLY represent the Cfm of stack gas, under usual conditions, that an induced draft fan would have to handle?

    A. X   B. 2X   C. 3X   D. 4X

24. If the stack switch of an oil burner becomes excessively sooted, a condition that is MOST likely to result is

    A. continuous shutting down of the burner shortly after it starts up
    B. excessive flow of oil to the burner resulting in a smoky fire
    C. excessive fire due to failure to cut off current to the burner motor
    D. failure of the warp switch of the relay to operate

25. In the usual high pressure electric generating plant in large buildings, heating the feedwater from 70° F to 180° F with exhaust steam usually will *decrease* the fuel consumption by

    A. 5%   B. 10%   C. 15%   D. 20%

KEY (CORRECT ANSWERS)

1. D		11. B	
2. B		12. D	
3. A		13. B	
4. B		14. B	
5. D		15. C	
6. C		16. D	
7. B		17. D	
8. D		18. D	
9. D		19. B	
10. C		20. B	

21. A
22. C
23. B
24. A
25. B

EXAMINATION SECTION
TEST 1

DIRECTIONS: Each question or incomplete statement is followed by several suggested answers or completions. Select the one that BEST answers the question or completes the statement. *PRINT THE LETTER OF THE CORRECT ANSWER IN THE SPACE AT THE RIGHT.*

1. Cast-iron heating boilers that are shipped in sections are USUALLY assembled on the job location with

    A. stud bolts and nuts
    B. push nipples and tie rods
    C. anchor bolts
    D. stay bolts

    1.____

2. In a two-pipe mechanical condensate-return system, the two valves that are installed in the discharge piping between the condensate pump and boiler are a _____ valve and _____ check valve.

    A. gate; swing
    B. globe; lift
    C. gate; lift
    D. globe; swing

    2.____

3. When a thermostatic trap is used in a steam supply heating system, the *cooling leg* must be installed

    A. between the equipment or drip and the thermostatic trap
    B. after the thermostatic trap
    C. at an angle of 45° to the main
    D. below the water line of the boiler

    3.____

4. The essential features of construction of a Hartford Loop connection to a steam heating boiler are a direct connection between the steam side and return side of the boiler and a _____ from the return main to the return side of the boiler.

    A. long nipple connection two inches above the normal water line
    B. close nipple connection two inches below the normal water line
    C. valved (gate) connection
    D. connection at the water level

    4.____

5. *Unit trapping* of two or more steam-consuming condensing units is recommended to

    A. allow for expansion of pipes
    B. eliminate check valves
    C. prevent the build-up of condensate and air in one or more units
    D. increase the back pressure on each unit

    5.____

6. Packless type steam radiator supply valves are recommended for use in _____ heating systems.

    A. two-pipe vacuum
    B. two-pipe vapor
    C. one-pipe gravity air-vent
    D. two-pipe gravity air-vent

    6.____

7. Of the following types of high-pressure steam piping systems, the one which is WIDELY used in small and medium-sized plants is the _____ system.

    A. single-header B. spider
    C. loop or ring D. unit

8. Compressed-air systems in power plants USUALLY operate at pressures of _____ psig.

    A. 30 to 40   B. 50 to 60   C. 70 to 90   D. 100 to 125

9. A *return header* is used on a cast-iron sectional boiler to distribute the condensate to both rear tappings.
   Of the following fittings, the ones that should be used where the branch connections enter the return tappings are

    A. elbows B. full size plugged tees
    C. reducer couplings D. bull head tees

10. The MINIMUM pitch for horizontal runouts to risers and heating units in a two-pipe high-pressure steam system should be

    A. 1/4 inch in 10 feet B. 1/8 inch per foot
    C. 1/4 inch per foot D. 1/2 inch per foot

11. The air suction intake of an air compressor has to be relocated 30 feet further from the compressor than present location.
    In connection with this work, it would be recommended practice to

    A. install a drip at mid-point of the extended suction line
    B. increase the capacity of the air storage tank
    C. increase the diameter of the suction line piping
    D. install a relief valve immediately before the intake of the air compressor

12. Of the following statements pertaining to steam-supplied blast heaters, the one which is INCORRECT is that

    A. steam mains should be dripped into the heater sections
    B. return piping from heater to trap should be of the same size as the heater outlet connection
    C. return piping should not be run to an overhead main which is above the heater return connection
    D. steam piping and heater sections should be supported independently

13. A hot water heating line has to be offset to clearn an obstruction.
    Of the following combinations of fittings, the one which will offer the LEAST resistance to the flow of hot water is

    A. two 90° standard elbows and a short nipple
    B. two tees, with one run of each tee plugged, and a short nipple
    C. a 90° standard elbow, a 90° long turn elbow, and a short nipple
    D. two 90° long turn elbows and a short nipple

14. The inlet piping to each heating unit in a two-pipe vapor steam heating system should be equipped with a(n) _____ valve.

    A. gate
    B. modulating
    C. OS & Y
    D. check

15. Of the following piping materials, the one that should NOT be used in a fuel-oil piping system is

    A. steel pipe
    B. brass pipe
    C. type K copper tubing
    D. galvanized iron

16. Assume that a shut-off valve is installed in the discharge line from an oil pump. In this installation, the valve that should be installed between the oil pump and the shut-off valve is a _____ valve.

    A. swing check
    B. globe
    C. relief
    D. air

17. A pump is to be raised 1/2" above its bed-plate. One 1/4" plate and one 3/16" plate are used.
    The number of 1/64" shims that must be used in addition to the 1/4" and 3/16" plates is

    A. 4
    B. 7
    C. 11
    D. 20

18. If 250 feet of 4" pipe weighs 400 pounds, the weight of this pipe per linear foot is _____ pounds.

    A. 1.25
    B. 1.50
    C. 1.60
    D. 1.75

19. The proper designation for a tee fitting which has on the *run* a 1 1/2" pipe thread and a 2" pipe thread with the *branch* having a 1" pipe thread is

    A. 1" x 1 1/2" x 2"
    B. 1 1/2" x 1" x 2"
    C. 2" x 1" x 1 1/2"
    D. 2" x 1 1/2" x 1"

20. Taper-tapped couplings are recommended for _____ piping.

    A. low-pressure gas
    B. high-pressure steam
    C. vent
    D. potable water supply

21. A steam heating system that operates both in vacuum and under low-pressure (0 to 15 psig) conditions without the use of a vacuum pump is known as a _____ system.

    A. high-pressure
    B. low-pressure
    C. vapor
    D. vacuum

22. A flange joint in a high-temperature piping system has to be broken frequently. To prevent the gasket from sticking to the flange face, it is GOOD practice to coat the gasket with

    A. high-grade epoxy
    B. water-resistant grease
    C. graphite
    D. talc

23. Pipe dope is applied to the male threads and not to the female threads when making-up a screwed pipe joint. The MAIN reason for this is to

    A. compensate for not using wicking
    B. prevent contamination of the fluid in the piping system

C. save on pipe dope material and labor
D. reduce friction when pulling-up the joint

24. Flanged faces of steel valves and fittings are NORMALLY manufactured with _____ flange face(s).

    A. raised
    B. plain
    C. flat
    D. one end having a raised flange face and the other end a plain

25. Regulating or throttling valves are SELDOM used in sizes above

    A. 12"   B. 15"   C. 18"   D. 20"

26. An 80' steam heating main is being piped up.
    If the pitch (fall) is 1/4" in 10 feet, and the centerline elevation at the beginning of the run is 9.989 feet, then the centerline elevation, in feet, at the lower end of the run is MOST NEARLY

    A. 11.989   B. 10.156   C. 9.822   D. 7.989

27. A set of heating plan drawings is drawn to a scale of 1/4" = 1 foot.
    If a length of pipe measures 4 5/8" on the drawing, the actual length of the pipe, in feet, is

    A. 16.3   B. 16.8   C. 17.5   D. 18.5

28. Of the following pastes, the one which is NOT suitable for making up threads in oil piping is

    A. red glyptol
    B. litharge and glycerin
    C. white or red lead oil paste
    D. permatex

29. Of the following valves, the one which is used for preventing the reversal of flow in a pipe is the _____ valve.

    A. check   B. globe
    C. pressure-regulating   D. gate

30. Of the following fittings, the one that is used to connect a 1 1/4" pipe directly to a 1" pipe in a straight line is called a

    A. union   B. sleeve   C. reducer   D. nipple

31. The pipe diameter of header drips installed in a high-pressure steam piping system USUALLY ranges from

    A. 1/4" to 1/2"   B. 3/4" to 1"
    C. 1 1/2" to 1 3/4"   D. 2" to 2 1/2"

32. Of the following types of gasket material, the types that should be used between flanges on a pipe conveying 900° F hot water is

   A. red rubber or neoprene
   B. fiber or paper
   C. copper, corrugated or plain
   D. steel, corrugated or plain

33. The MAIN reason for installing a by-pass line around a 10" high-pressure gate valve is to

   A. make it easier to close the valve
   B. make it easier to open the valve
   C. reduce the steam-line pressure
   D. tap off steam for other uses

34. Of the following valves, the one that is considered a *dead end* type of valve is a _____ valve.

   A. single-seated pressure-reducing
   B. double-seated pressure-reducing
   C. high-pressure steam-throttling
   D. relief

35. A valve is marked *600 WOG.*
    This valve could NOT be properly used in a pipe conveying _____ pounds gage maximum.

   A. water at 500
   B. oil at 600
   C. air at 300
   D. steam at 600

36. Flange dimensions and materials are established by the

   A. ASA (American Standards Association) *Code for Pressure Piping*
   B. ASME (American Society of Mechanical Engineers) *Boiler Code*
   C. NDHA (National District Heating Association) *Piping Code*
   D. NBS (National Bureau of Standards) *Piping Materials Code*

37. A steam leak in a pipe line allows steam to escape at a rate of 50,000 pounds each month.
    Assuming that the cost of steam is 50 cents per 1,000 pounds, the total cost of wasted steam from this leak for a 12-month period would amount to

   A. $25   B. $60   C. $300   D. $600

38. Of the following, the method which is MOST likely to give an accurate reading in checking a 0-to-400 psig pressure gage is to

   A. adjust the pointer to zero
   B. connect the gage and a *test gage* to a pressure line in which the pressures may be varied, and compare the readings of the two gages
   C. use a dead-weight gage tester
   D. connect the gage to a steam line and compare the pressure reading with another gage installed on the same steam line

39. An oil separator in a non-condensing steam plant removes oil from 39.____

    A. live steam   B. feedwater
    C. exhaust steam   D. condensate

40. The MAIN function of a double offset U-bend in a high-pressure steam line is to 40.____

    A. protect pressure gages
    B. reverse the steam flow
    C. permit expansion of the steam line
    D. by-pass a trap or valve

KEY (CORRECT ANSWERS)

1. B	11. C	21. C	31. B
2. A	12. A	22. C	32. D
3. A	13. D	23. B	33. B
4. B	14. B	24. A	34. A
5. C	15. D	25. A	35. D
6. A	16. C	26. C	36. A
7. A	17. A	27. D	37. C
8. D	18. C	28. C	38. C
9. B	19. D	29. A	39. C
10. D	20. B	30. C	40. C

TEST 2

DIRECTIONS: Each question or incomplete statement is followed by several suggested answers or completions. Select the one that BEST answers the question or completes the statement. *PRINT THE LETTER OF THE CORRECT ANSWER IN THE SPACE AT THE RIGHT.*

1. The MINIMUM permitted diameter of the pipes connecting a water column to a power boiler is

   A. 1/4"   B. 3/8"   C. 3/4"   D. 1"

   1.____

2. A steam gage is installed above a steam pipe with a gooseneck siphon. The MAIN purpose of the gooseneck siphon is to

   A. maintain a water seal between the gage and steam supply
   B. drip condensate back into the steam pipeline
   C. allow for expansion of the connection
   D. eliminate vibrations

   2.____

3. The anemometer rating of a unit ventilator is USUALLY expressed in

   A. pounds per square inch   B. cubic feet per minute
   C. BTU/hour   D. pounds per hour

   3.____

4. In accordance with the ASME Code for Low Pressure Heating Boilers, the MAXIMUM allowable working pressure for a hot water heating boiler is _____ psi.

   A. 15   B. 30   C. 160   D. 250

   4.____

5. The MOST common device used for measuring steam consumption in a district heating system is the

   A. steam flow meter   B. condensate meter
   C. Bailey meter   D. manometer

   5.____

6. Of the following types of steam traps, the one which must be primed or filled with water prior to operation is the _____ trap.

   A. inverted-bucket   B. open or upright-bucket
   C. float   D. float-and-thermostatic

   6.____

7. Of the following types of steam traps, the one which is recommended for dripping the ends of steam mains is the _____ trap.

   A. float   B. inverted-bucket
   C. open or upright-bucket D. float-and-thermostatic

   7.____

8. The removal of carbon dioxide gas from a two-pipe system heating system is accomplished by the use of a

   A. blow-off connection on the boiler
   B. steam trap
   C. steam separator
   D. relief valve

   8.____

9. In a true packless-type steam radiator supply valve, leakage around the stem is prevented by a

   A. regular packing nut
   B. diaphragm
   C. metal bellows
   D. packing gland

10. Of the following types of steam radiator supply valves, the one MOST generally used in a two-pipe steam heating system is the _____ type.

    A. straightway
    B. right-hand
    C. angle
    D. left-hand

11. The MAIN function of a *Copes Regulator* is to regulate the amount of

    A. steam leaving a boiler
    B. feedwater entering a boiler drum
    C. make up water leaving the closed feedwater heater
    D. steam pressure in a boiler drum

12. A device that could be used in a low-pressure hot water system which would help prevent air from entering the main is the

    A. relief valve
    B. dip tube
    C. circulating pump
    D. flow-check valve

13. The function of an *injector* in a steam plant is to

    A. supply fuel oil to the burners
    B. spray water into the hot well
    C. drain the after cooler
    D. lift and force water into a boiler

14. Of the following knots, the one that is used to take the strain off the connections to an electrical plug is the

    A. square knot
    B. underwriter's knot
    C. clove hitch
    D. slip knot

15. The safety term *safe-ending* pertains MOST NEARLY to

    A. hammer-struck tools such as chisels or number dies
    B. circular saw blades
    C. large pipe wrenches
    D. pipe dies and reamers

16. Of the following types of portable fire extinguishers, the one which should be used on a *live* electrical fire is the _____ type.

    A. foam
    B. carbon dioxide
    C. soda-acid
    D. water

17. The MAIN reason for using a three-pronged plug with portable electrical tools is to

    A. decrease the amperage rating of the fuse
    B. provide a means to conserve electrical energy
    C. increase the line voltage
    D. ground them properly

18. The total length of four pieces of pipe whose lengths are 3 ft. 4 1/2 in., 2 ft. 1 5/16 in., 4 ft. 9 3/8 in., and 2 ft. 3 1/4 in., respectively, is   18.____

    A. 11 ft. 5 7/16" B. 11 ft. 6 7/16"
    C. 12 ft. 5 7/16" D. 12 ft. 6 7/16"

19. The DESIRABLE feature of a ratchet wrench is that it   19.____

    A. can exert more force than an open-end wrench
    B. does not damage the nut
    C. can be used in a limited space without removing the wrench from the nut
    D. will not strip the threads

20. A drift punch is used to   20.____

    A. tighten small rivets
    B. set escutcheon pin heads
    C. enlarge small holes
    D. drive out pins

21. Of the following tools, the one which it is BEST to use to remove burrs from the inside of a pipe is a(n)   21.____

    A. auger bit B. diamond-point chisel
    C. pillar file D. reamer

22. The tool or device which should be used to bore a hole in a concrete wall is a   22.____

    A. round-nose drill B. diamond-point chisel
    C. center punch D. star drill

23. Of the following wrenches, the one which is the MOST suitable and fastest to work with when pulling up flange bolts and nuts is a(n) _____ wrench.   23.____

    A. open-end or socket B. monkey or hex
    C. pipe D. chain pipe

24. Assume that a pipe threading die has a set of 4 chasers and the heel clearance of the chaser threads is worn away.   24.____
    Of the following actions, the BEST one to take would be to have the

    A. lip rake angle re-ground
    B. cutting angle re-ground
    C. lead angle beveled
    D. set replaced

25. Of the following sizes of pipe wrenches, the one that is GENERALLY used to make up 3/4" or 1" diameter pipe is   25.____

    A. 18" B. 10" C. 8" D. 6"

26. A 1:3:5 concrete mix is a mixture consisting of 1 part _____, 3 parts _____, and 5 parts _____.   26.____

    A. gravel, cement, sand B. cement, sand, gravel
    C. gravel, sand, cement D. sand, cement, gravel

27. D. low-pressure return
28. A. flanged
29. D. float and thermostatic
30. C. support or hanger
31. A. condensate
32. A. 12
33. B. $4,000

Questions 34-36.

DIRECTIONS: Questions 34 through 36, inclusive, are to be answered in accordance with the following par

The heat output from unit heaters will depend on how fast and how completely dry hot steam fills the unit core. For complete and fast air removal and rapid drainage of condensate, use a trap actuated by water or vapor (inverted bucket trap) .and not a trap operated by temperature only (thermostatic or bellows trap). A temperature-actuated trap will hold back the hot condensate until it cools to a point where the thermal element opens. When this happens,, the condensate backs up in the heater and reduces the heat output. With a water-actuated trap, this will not happen, as the water or condensate is discharged as fast as it is formed.

34. On the basis of the information given in the above paragraph, it can be concluded that the proper type of trap to use for a unit heater is a(n) _____ trap. 34.____

    A. thermostatic
    B. bellows-type
    C. inverted bucket
    D. temperature

35. According to the above paragraph, the MAIN reason for using the type of trap specified for a unit heater is to 35.____

    A. bring the condensate up to steam temperature
    B. prevent reduction in the heat output of the unit heater
    C. permit cycling of the heater
    D. maintain constant temperature of condensate in the trap

36. As used in the above paragraph, the word *actuated* means MOST NEARLY 36.____

    A. clogged   B. operated   C. cleaned   D. vented

37. When supervising a helper, you should be 37.____

    A. fair in your actions towards him
    B. stern and to the point
    C. apologetic and condescending
    D. sarcastic and smart

38. Assume that a helper under your supervision disagrees with your evaluation of his work. Of the following statements, the one which describes the BEST way to handle the situation is to 38.____

    A. refuse to discuss his contention in order to maintain discipline
    B. advise him that the other men are satisfied with your evaluation and he has no right to complain
    C. explain to him that since you have more working experience, you are more able to evaluate his work than he is
    D. explain the basis of your evaluation and discuss it with him

39. The MAIN responsibility of anyone who has men working under him is to 39.____
   A. make himself liked and respected by his men.
   B. see that all his men are treated the same when duties are assigned
   C. create an attitude in his men which will be receptive toward policies of the department
   D. get the work done properly

40. The BEST way of giving directions to a helper, is to 40.____
   A. lay out a rough plan of procedure and see if the helper has the intelligence to work out his own method
   B. give only general hints of how you want the work accomplished
   C. be exact and omit none of the essential points
   D. question the helper frequently to determine if he thinks that you have given him sufficient information

KEY (CORRECT ANSWERS)

1. D	11. B	21. D	31. A
2. A	12. B	22. D	32. A
3. B	13. D	23. A	33. B
4. C	14. B	24. D	34. C
5. B	15. A	25. A	35. B
6. A	16. B	26. B	36. B
7. D	17. D	27. B	37. A
8. B	18. D	28. B	38. D
9. C	19. C	29. D	39. D
10. C	20. D	30. C	40. C

EXAMINATION SECTION
TEST 1

DIRECTIONS: Each question or incomplete statement is followed by several suggested answers or completions. Select the one that BEST answers the question or completes the statement. *PRINT THE LETTER OF THE CORRECT ANSWER IN THE SPACE AT THE RIGHT.*

1. The MOST commonly used fuel gas is 1.____
   A. butane   B. propane   C. acetylene   D. methane

2. Oxygen is used in conjunction with a fuel gas in order to 2.____
   A. reduce the temperatures generated
   B. support combustion
   C. make fuel gases safer to use
   D. decrease polluting effects

3. _____ creates the GREATEST amount of heat when burned. 3.____
   A. Propane   B. Methane   C. Butane   D. Acetylene

4. An oxyacetylene system uses _____ cylinder(s). 4.____
   A. two   B. three   C. four   D. one

5. Oxygen cylinders are made of 5.____
   A. aluminum   B. steel
   C. iron   D. all of the above

6. The percentage of oxygen in a cylinder is _____%. 6.____
   A. 50   B. 75   C. 90   D. 100

7. The pressures in oxygen cylinders can range up to ____ psi. 7.____
   A. 1500   B. 2000   C. 2200   D. 2500

8. Oxygen cylinders are ALWAYS painted 8.____
   A. green   B. blue   C. yellow   D. black

9. Acetylene cylinders are ALWAYS painted 9.____
   A. green   B. blue   C. yellow   D. black

10. Inside an acetylene cylinder, there is 10.____
    A. acetylene   B. acetone
    C. honeycomb material   D. all of the above

11. It is extremely dangerous to use acetylene at pressures above _____ psi. 11.____
    A. 15   B. 25   C. 100   D. 250

12. Pure acetylene is _____ when compressed.

    A. safe   B. explosive   C. a solid   D. cold

13. Both acetylene and oxygen cylinders have

    A. control valves
    B. regulators
    C. safety features
    D. all of the above

14. Acetylene cylinders contain both regulators and _____ as safety devices.

    A. limiters
    B. fusible plugs
    C. valves
    D. caps

15. Portable systems are USUALLY secured to a

    A. shoulder harness
    B. hydraulic cart
    C. handtruck
    D. backpack

16. Both oxygen and acetylene cylinders should ALWAYS be kept in a(n) _____ position.

    A. upright
    B. horizontal
    C. inverted
    D. suspended

17. A manifold oxyacetylene system is often used when work is

    A. done in several different locations
    B. always done in the workshop
    C. always done at the same stations in the workshop
    D. primarily heating and brazing

18. Oxygen and acetylene are mixed inside the

    A. hoses
    B. regulator
    C. torch
    D. all of the above

19. Regulators control

    A. internal cylinder pressure
    B. discharge pressure
    C. mixing volume
    D. all of the above

20. Regulators are _____ adjusted.

    A. automatically
    B. pneumatically
    C. manually
    D. hydraulically

21. _____ are used to protect the cylinder valves when not in use.

    A. Caps   B. Cradles   C. Cushions   D. Covers

22. A special key is needed to

    A. open the acetylene cylinder
    B. attach the hoses
    C. adjust the flame
    D. adjust the gas mixture

23. The oxyacetylene mixture is _____ ignited. 23._____
    A. automatically
    B. manually
    C. spontaneously
    D. none of the above

24. The GREATEST fire hazard occurring during the use of oxyacetylene equipment is from 24._____
    A. the extremely hot flame
    B. a cylinder explosion
    C. sparks and hot metals
    D. unexpected heating of combustibles

25. Sparks and hot metal cause APPROXIMATELY _____% of all fires during torch operations. 25._____
    A. 25
    B. 50
    C. 60
    D. 75

KEY (CORRECT ANSWERS)

1. C
2. B
3. D
4. A
5. B

6. D
7. C
8. A
9. D
10. D

11. A
12. B
13. D
14. B
15. C

16. A
17. C
18. C
19. B
20. C

21. A
22. A
23. B
24. C
25. C

TEST 2

DIRECTIONS: Each question or incomplete statement is followed by several suggested answers or completions. Select the one that BEST answers the question or completes the statement. *PRINT THE LETTER OF THE CORRECT ANSWER IN THE SPACE AT THE RIGHT.*

1. All torch operators and fireguards must hold a(n) 1.____

    A. operator's license
    B. certificate of fitness
    C. CPR and first aid certificate
    D. all of the above

2. The above document must be _____ during all torch operations. 2.____

    A. in the operator's possession
    B. on file with the state
    C. on file with the county
    D. on file with the operator's employer

3. _____ fireguard(s) is(are) required for each torch operator. 3.____

    A. One   B. Two   C. Three   D. Four

4. An additional fireguard is required 4.____

    A. to circulate between welding stations
    B. on the floor below the work area
    C. on the floor above the work area
    D. all of the above

5. The supervisor must 5.____

    A. be notified in writing 48 hours before work is done
    B. designate a safe work area
    C. provide a copy of the building safety regulations
    D. all of the above

6. The supervisor may NOT be 6.____

    A. the cutting or welding contractor
    B. an employee of the building owner
    C. allowed into the cutting or welding station
    D. all of the above

7. All of the following are of concern to the supervisor EXCEPT 7.____

    A. open duct work or vents
    B. combustible materials
    C. partially filled acetylene cylinders
    D. none of the above

8. Oxyacetylene equipment should be approved by

   A. OSHA
   B. the Board of Standards and Appeals
   C. the supervisor
   D. all of the above

9. Safety clothing includes all of the following EXCEPT

   A. protective goggles
   B. fire-resistant gauntlet gloves
   C. an open collar shirt with protective pockets
   D. none of the above

10. All of the following present fire hazards during welding operations EXCEPT

    A. flammable gases   B. paper
    C. asbestos insulation   D. plywood boards

11. The work area should be checked _____ after all torch work is completed.

    A. once   B. twice
    C. three times   D. every hour for six hours

12. A signed inspection report must be completed by

    A. each fireguard
    B. the supervisor
    C. a fire department inspector
    D. the torch operator

13. In order to prevent sprinkler heads from opening during routine torch work, they should be

    A. turned off at the standpipe head
    B. sprayed with water
    C. covered with wet rags
    D. all of the above

14. No flammable materials should be within _____ feet of the work area.

    A. 10   B. 25   C. 50   D. 100

15. All of the following are fire hazards EXCEPT flammable

    A. liquids   B. solids
    C. dusts   D. none of the above

16. Cylinder fittings should be greased

    A. weekly   B. monthly
    C. every six months   D. never

17. The presence of _____ makes materials more likely to ignite.

    A. heat   B. oxygen
    C. acetylene   D. all of the above

18. Oxygen and acetylene should be stored in _____ enclosures.

    A. locked, airtight   B. well-ventilated
    C. separate   D. air-conditioned

19. Oxygen cylinders should have _____ regulators.

    A. green   B. red   C. gray   D. black

20. Acetylene cylinders should have _____ regulators.

    A. green   B. red   C. gray   D. black

21. Oxygen regulators and hose fittings have _____ threads.

    A. right-hand   B. left-hand
    C. universal   D. all of the above

22. Acetylene regulators and hose fittings have _____ threads.

    A. left-hand   B. right-hand
    C. universal   D. all of the above

23. The oxygen cylinder should be opened _____ when preparing to begin work.

    A. one half turn   B. one full turn
    C. one and one-half turns   D. completely

24. The acetylene cylinder should be opened _____ when preparing to begin work.

    A. one half turn   B. one full turn
    C. one and one half turns   D. completely

25. To INCREASE the amount of acetylene used during an operation,

    A. gradually increase the pressure
    B. open the valve in one half turn increments
    C. use a larger diameter hose
    D. all of the above

KEY (CORRECT ANSWERS)

1.	B		11.	B
2.	A		12.	A
3.	A		13.	C
4.	B		14.	B
5.	D		15.	D
6.	A		16.	D
7.	C		17.	D
8.	B		18.	C
9.	C		19.	A
10.	C		20.	B

21. A
22. A
23. D
24. B
25. C

TEST 3

DIRECTIONS: Each question or incomplete statement is followed by several suggested answers or completions. Select the one that BEST answers the question or completes the statement. *PRINT THE LETTER OF THE CORRECT ANSWER IN THE SPACE AT THE RIGHT.*

1. Before use, the valves on both the oxygen and acetylene cylinders should be   1.____

   A. lubricated with a mineral oil
   B. wiped clean
   C. moistened with a damp cloth
   D. all of the above

2. Before attaching the regulators, both cylinder valves should be opened for an instant in order to   2.____

   A. check the pressure
   B. prime the cylinders
   C. clear any dirt blocking the valve outlets
   D. all of the above

3. Control valves on the torch should be opened   3.____

   A. before the regulators are adjusted
   B. after the regulators are adjusted
   C. to establish the desired pressures
   D. to decrease pressure when the regulator is attached

4. Of the following, the CORRECT order for removing equipment from the cylinders is   4.____

   A. close oxygen and acetylene cylinder valves, bleed hoses, open pressure adjusting screw, remove regulator
   B. open pressure adjusting screw, bleed hoses, close oxygen and acetylene cylinder valves, remove regulator
   C. close oxygen and acetylene cylinder valves, open pressure adjusting screw, bleed valves, remove regulator
   D. none of the above

5. The term *backfire* refers to   5.____

   A. the flame burning inside the torch or hoses
   B. an insufficient charge in the cylinders
   C. a torch going out unexpectedly
   D. all of the above

6. Possible causes for backfire do NOT include   6.____

   A. the nozzle tip touching the work surface
   B. a loose or dirty nozzle tip
   C. dirt on the work surface
   D. inadequate ventilation

7. The term *flashback* refers to

   A. the flame burning inside the torch or hoses
   B. an insufficient charge in the cylinders
   C. a torch going out unexpectedly
   D. an oxyacetylene induced hallucination

8. Of the following, the type of leak that is EASILY detected is an _____ leak.

   A. oxygen   B. acetylene
   C. both of the above   D. none of the above

9. Leaks should be checked for using a(n)

   A. electronic detector   B. halide torch detector
   C. soap and water solution D. all of the above

10. An acceptable means of repairing hoses is by _____ the affected area.

    A. cutting and splicing   B. taping
    C. heating   D. all of the above

11. _____ tubing should NEVER be used with acetylene.

    A. Rubber   B. Plastic
    C. Copper   D. None of the above

12. Gas cylinders that are stored should be protected from

    A. snow   B. rust
    C. direct sunlight D. all of the above

13. Oxygen cylinders should be stored AT LEAST feet from any combustible materials.

    A. 25   B. 50   C. 75   D. 100

14. Using oxyacetylene equipment in manholes or other underground structures is particularly hazardous due to

    A. poor lighting
    B. the potential build-up of flammable gas or liquids
    C. unsanitary conditions
    D. the likely presence of water

15. Of the following, the MOST care should be taken to adequately _____ underground structures.

    A. dry   B. ventilate   C. light   D. heat

16. Liquids and gases that build up in manholes may be

    A. toxic   B. suffocating
    C. flammable   D. all of the above

17. If the oxygen content in a structure is below _____%, workers may not enter unless equipped with a self-contained breathing apparatus.

    A. 19.5   B. 25.5   C. 50   D. 56.5

18. Of the following, the MOST common solder used in jewelry manufacturing is

    A. gold B. tin C. lead D. copper

19. When *soft soldering,* the torch flame is below _____ ° F.

    A. 600 B. 800 C. 1000 D. 1200

20. Fuel gases that are used in jewelry manufacture do NOT include

    A. propane B. butane
    C. acetylene D. none of the above

21. The only person REQUIRED to hold a certificate of fitness for torch operations in a jewelry manufacturing plant is the

    A. torch operator
    B. supervisor of torch operations
    C. fireguard
    D. owner of the plant

22. Fire extinguishers must be inspected every

    A. 6 months B. year C. two years D. three years

23. Air for the torches used in jewelry manufacture may be supplied by all of the following means EXCEPT

    A. compressor B. bellows
    C. mouth D. fan

24. The certificate of fitness holder is REQUIRED to know the

    A. location and operation of all installed fire extinguishing devices
    B. location of any fire alarm stations
    C. telephone number of the fire department borough communications office
    D. all of the above

25. Fire extinguishers may contain all of the following extinguishing agents EXCEPT

    A. water B. carbon dioxide
    C. oxygen D. dry chemicals

KEY (CORRECT ANSWERS)

1. B
2. C
3. B
4. A
5. C

6. D
7. A
8. B
9. C
10. A

11. C
12. D
13. A
14. B
15. B

16. D
17. A
18. A
19. C
20. D

21. B
22. A
23. D
24. D
25. C

BASIC FUNDAMENTALS OF BOILERS

TABLE OF CONTENTS

		Page
I.	NATURE	1
II.	CLASSIFICATION	2
	A. Location of Fire and Water Spaces	2
	B. Size of Tubes	2
	C. Type of Circulation	2
	D. Type of Superheat	3
III.	TERMINOLOGY	3
	A. Fire Room and Boiler Room	4
	B. Boiler Emergency Station	4
	C. Boiler Full-Power Capacity	4
	D. Boiler Overload Capacity	4
	E. Superheater Outlet Pressure	4
	F. Steam Drum Pressure	4
	G. Design Pressure	4
	H. Operating Pressure	4
	I. Boiler Efficiency	4
	J. Fire Room Efficiency	4
	K. Total Heating Surface	5
	L. Generating Surface	5
	M. Superheater Surface	5
	N. Economizer Surface	5
	O. Steaming Hours	5

BASIC FUNDAMENTALS OF BOILERS

I. NATURE

The boiler is the source or high-temperature region of the thermos-dynamic cycle. The steam that is generated in the boiler is led to the turbines, where its thermal energy is converted into mechanical energy (work) which drives the unit and provides power for vital services.

In essence, a boiler is merely a container in which water can be boiled and steam generated. A tea kettle on a stove is basically a boiler, although a rather inefficient one. Note that the steam is generated in one vessel and superheated in another, since it is impossible to raise the temperature of the steam above the temperature of the boiling water as long as the two are in contact with each other.

In designing a boiler which must produce a large amount of steam, it is obviously necessary to find some means of providing a larger amount of heat-transfer surface than could be provided by a vessel shaped like a tea kettle. In most modern boilers, the steam generating surface consists of hundreds and hundreds of tubes, which provide a maximum amount of heat-transfer surface in a relatively small space. As a rule, the tubes communicate with a steam drum at the top of a boiler and with water drums and headers at the bottom of the boiler. The tubes and part of the drums are enclosed in an insulated capsule which has space inside it for the furnace. A boiler appears to be a fairly complicated piece of equipment when it is considered with all its fittings, piping, and accessories; it may be helpful, therefore, to remember that the basic components of a saturated-steam boiler are merely the tubes, the drums, and headers, and the furnace.

Practically all boilers used in propulsion are designed to produce both saturated steam and superheated steam. To our basic boiler, therefore, we must now add another component: the superheater. The superheater on most boilers consist of headers, usually located at the back of the boiler, and a number of superheater tubes which communicate with the headers. Saturated steam from the steam drum is led through the superheater; since the steam is now no longer in contact with the water from which it was generated, the steam becomes superheated as additional heat is supplied. In some boilers, there is a separate superheater furnace; in others, the superheater tubes project into the same furnace that is used for the generation of saturated steam.

Some question may arise concerning the need for both saturated steam and superheated steam. Saturated steam is used for operating most steam-driven auxiliary machinery; reciprocating machinery, in particular, requires saturated steam for the lubrication of the moving parts of the steam end. Superheated steam is used almost exclusively for the propulsion turbines. There is more available energy in superheated steam than in saturated steam at the same pressure; and the use of higher temperatures vastly increases the efficiency of the propulsion cycle since, as we have seen, the efficiency of a heat engine is dependent upon the absolute temperature at the source (boiler) and the absolute temperature at the receiver (condenser). In some instances, the gain in efficiency resulting from the use of superheated steam may be as much as 15 percent for 200 degrees of superheat. This increase in efficiency is particularly important because it allows substantial

can be carried by the downcomer. The size and number of downcomers installed varies from one type of boiler to another.

Forced circulation boilers are, as their name implies, quite different in design from the boilers that utilize natural circulation. Instead of depending upon differences in density between the hotter and the cooler water, forced circulation boilers use pumps to force the water through the various boiler circuits. Forced circulation boilers are relatively new, but they have some very definite advantages which will probably lead to their increased use in the future.

D. Type of Superheat

Practically all boilers are equipped with superheaters. With respect to the superheater installation, boilers are classified as having either controlled superheat or uncontrolled superheat. In a boiler with *controlled superheat*, the degree of superheat can be changed by regulating the amount of heat supplied to the superheater tube bank, without substantially changing the amount of heat supplied to the generating tubes. This control of superheat is possible because the boiler has two furnaces, one for the saturated side and one for the superheat side. A boiler with *uncontrolled superheat*, on the other hand, has only one furnace; and since the same furnace must be used for heating both the generating tubes and the superheater tubes, the degree of superheat cannot be controlled but varies within a small range as a function of design and firing rate.

Various terms are used to describe these two basic types of superheaters. Where the superheat is controlled, the superheater is often referred to as an *integral, separately fired superheat*, and the boiler as a whole is called a *superheat control boiler*. Where the superheat is not controlled, the superheater may be called an *integral, not separately fired superheater*, or it may be referred to as a *no control, or uncontrolled superheater*; and the boiler as a whole is called a *no control or uncontrolled superheat boiler*. The term *integral* is used to indicate that the superheater is installed as a part of the boiler unit. Practically all superheaters on modern boilers are integral with the boilers.

On both controlled and uncontrolled superheat boilers, the superheater tubes are protected from radiant heat by generation tubes that are called *water screen tubes*. The water screen tubes absorb the intense radiant heat of the furnace, and the superheater tubes are heated by convection currents rather than by direct radiation. Hence, the superheaters are sometimes called *convection-type superheaters*.

Some older types of superheat control boilers had *radiant-type superheaters*—that is, the superheater tubes were not screened by water tubes but were exposed directly to the radiant heat of the furnace. However, this type of superheater is relatively uncommon at the present time and will, therefore, not be further discussed.

III. TERMINOLOGY

In order to ensure uniform use of terms, there has been established a number of standard terms and definitions pertaining to boilers. Some of the more important of these definitions are given below.

savings in fuel consumption and in space and weight requirements. A
using superheated steam for propulsion machinery is that it causes rela
since it is free of moisture

II. CLASSIFICATION

Boilers may be classified in a number of different ways, according to various d
features. Most commonly, they are classified and described in terms of (1) the
location of the fire and water spaces, (2) the size of the tubes, (3) the type of circ
(4) the type of superheat. Some knowledge of these methods of classification will
in understanding the design and construction of modern boilers.

A. Location of Fire and Water Spaces

First of all, boilers are classified according to the relative location of their fire and wat
spaces. By this classification, all boilers may be divided into two groups: *fire-tube boilers* and *water-tube boilers*. In *fire-tube boilers*, the gases of combustion flow throug
the tubes and thereby heat the surrounding water. In *water-tube boilers*, the water flows
through the tubes and is heated by the gases of combustion that fill the furnace.

B. Size of Tubes

Water-tube boilers are further classified according to the size of the tubes. Boilers
having tubes 2 inches or more in diameter are called *large-tube boilers*. Boilers having
tubes less than 2 inches in diameter are called *small-tube* or *express-type boilers*.

C. Type of Circulation

Water-tube boilers are also classified as *natural circulation boilers* or as *force circulation boilers*, depending upon the way in which the water circulates within the boiler.

Natural circulation boilers are those in which the circulation of water depends upon the
difference in density between an ascending mixture of hot water and steam and a
descending body of relatively cool and steam-free water. Natural circulation may be of
two types, free or accelerated.

In this type of boiler, the generating tubes are installed at a slight angle of inclination
which allows the lighter hot water and steam to rise while the cooler (and heavier) water
descends.

Installing the generating tubes at a greater angle of inclination increases the rate of
water circulation. Hence, boilers in which the tubes slope more steeply are said to have
accelerated natural circulation.

Most modern boilers are designed for accelerated natural circulation. In such boilers,
large tubes (3 or more inches in diameter) are installed between the steam drum and the
water drums. These tubes, called *downcomers*, are located outside the furnace and
away from the heat of combustion, thereby serving as pathways for the downward flow
of relatively cool water. When a sufficient number of downcomers are installed, all small
tubes can be generating tubes, carrying steam and water upward; and all downward flow

A. Fire Room and Boiler Room: A compartment which contains boilers and the station for operating them is called a *fire room*. A compartment which contains boilers which does not contain the station for operating them is called a *boiler room*.

B. Boiler Emergency Station: This term is used to designate a station which is so located that, in the event of trouble, one may proceed with minimum delay to any fire room, boiler operating station, or boiler room.

C. Boiler Full-Power Capacity: The total quantity of steam required to develop contract shaft horsepower of the vessel, divided by the number of boilers installed, gives boiler full-power capacity. The quantity of steam is given in pounds of water evaporated per hour. Full-power capacity is indicated in the manufacturer's technical manual for each boiler.

D. Boiler Overload Capacity: Boiler overload capacity is specified in the design of the boiler. It is given in terms of steaming rate or firing rate, depending upon the individual installation. Boiler overload capacity is usually 120 percent of boiler full-power capacity.

E. Superheater Outlet Pressure: This is the actual steam pressure at the superheater outlet.

F. Steam Drum Pressure: This is the pressure in the steam drum. Steam drum pressure is specified in the design of a boiler and is given in the manufacturer's technical manual for each boiler. Steam drum pressure is the pressure which must be carried in the boiler steam drum in order to obtain the required pressure at the turbine throttles, when steaming at full-power capacity. Ordinarily, the designed steam drum pressure is carried for all steaming conditions.

G. Design Pressure: Design pressure is the pressure specified by the boiler manufacturer as a criterion for boiler design. It is usually 103 percent of steam drum pressure.

H. Operating Pressure: Operating pressure is the pressure at the final outlet from a boiler, after steam has passed through all baffles, the dry pipe, the superheater, etc., when the boiler is steaming at full-power capacity. Operating pressure is specified in the design of a boiler and is given in the manufacturer's technical manual. Operating pressure is the same as superheater outlet pressure when the boiler is steaming at full-power capacity; when the boiler is steaming at less than full-power capacity, however, the actual pressure at the superheater outlet will vary from the specified operating pressure provided a constant drum pressure is maintained.

I. Boiler Efficiency: The efficiency of a boiler is the British thermal units per pound of fuel absorbed by the water and steam divided by the British thermal units per pound of fuel fired. In other words, boiler efficiency is output divided by input, or Btu utilized divided by Btu available. Boiler efficiency is expressed as a percentage.

J. Fire Room Efficiency: The boiler efficiency corrected for blower and pump steam consumption is known as fire room efficiency. (This is not the same as boiler plant efficiency or propulsion plant efficiency.)

K. Total Heating Surface: The total heating surface of any steam generating unit consists of that portion of the heat transfer apparatus which is exposed on one side to the gases of combustion and on the other side to the water or steam being heated. Thus, the total heating surface equals the sum of the generating surface, the superheater surface, and the economizer surface. All heating surfaces are measured on the combustion-gas side.

L. Generating Surface: The generating surface is that portion of the total heating surface in which the fluid being heated forms part of the circulating system. The generating surface includes the boiler tube banks, water walls, water screens, and water floors (where installed and not covered by refractory material.)

M. Superheater Surface: The superheater surface is that portion of the total heating surface where the steam is heated after leaving the boiler steam drum.

N. Economizer Surface: The economizer surface is that portion of the total heating surface where the feed water is heated before entering the generating system.

O. Steaming Hours: The term steaming hours includes the time during which the boiler has fires lighted for raising steam and the time during which it is generating steam. Time during which fires are not lighted is not included in steaming hours.

ENGINEERING FUNDAMENTALS

TABLE OF CONTENTS

		Page
I.	PHYSICS	1
	A. Mass, Weight and Inertia	1
	B. Force	1
	C. Speed, Velocity and Acceleration	1
	D. Energy	2
	E. Work	2
	F. Power	3
	G. Laws of Gases	3
	H. Pressure and Vacuum	4
	I. Gage Pressure	4
	J. Atmospheric Pressure	4
	K. Vacuum	5
	L. Absolute Pressure	5
II.	PRINCIPLES OF HYDRAULICS	7
III.	PRINCIPLES OF PNEUMATICS	8
	A. Heat	8
	B. Units of Measurement	9
	C. Sensible Heat and Latent Heat	10
	D. Temperature	11
	E. Combustion	12
IV.	METALS	14

NOTES AND RESOURCES

ENGINEERING FUNDAMENTALS

This part is designed to acquaint you with various laws and phenomena of nature. Included is information pertaining to matter and energy, force and motion, heat and temperature, pressure, combustion, the laws of perfect gases, and some fundamental information about metals. The information provided here is general in nature; but it has been included to give you a better understanding of how or why engineering machinery operates or produces work. As you study this part, remember that anything that occupies space and has weight is called MATTER.

I. PHYSICS

The forces of physics and the laws of nature are at work in every single piece of machinery or equipment aboard ship. It is by these forces and laws that the machinery and equipment produce work.

A. MASS, WEIGHT, AND INERTIA

The physical principles of mass and inertia are involved in the design and operation of the heavy flywheels and bull gears that are at work in the ship's engineering plant. The great mass of the wheel tends to keep it rotating once it has been set in motion. The high inertia of the wheel keeps it from responding to small fluctuations in speed and thus helps to keep the engine running smoothly.

The mass and the weight of an object are not the same. The mass of an object is the quantity of matter which the object contains. The weight of the object is equal to the gravitational force with which the object is attracted to the earth. Inertia is that physical property which causes objects that are at rest to remain at rest, unless they are acted upon by some external force; and which causes objects moving at a constant velocity to continue moving at this constant velocity, and in the same direction, until acted upon by some external force.

B. FORCE

Force is what makes an object start to move, or speedup, or slow down; or keep moving against resistance. This force may be either a push or a pull. You exert a force when you push against a truck, whether you move the truck, or only try to move it. You also exert a force when you pull on a heavy piano, whether you move the piano, or only try to move it. Forces produce or prevent motion, or have a tendency to do so.

A tendency to prevent motion is the frictional resistance offered by an object. This frictional resistance is called frictional force. While it can never cause an object to move, it can check or stop motion. Frictional force wastes power, creates heat, and causes wear. Although frictional force cannot be entirely eliminated, it can be reduced by using lubricants.

C. SPEED, VELOCITY, AND ACCELERATION

Speed is defined as the distance covered per unit of time. Velocity is speed in a certain direction. Acceleration is the rate at which velocity changes. If, for example, the propeller shaft rate of rotation increases from stop to 100 revolutions per minute (rpm) in 20 minutes, the acceleration is 5 rpm. In other words, the velocity has increased 5 revolutions per minute, during each minute, for a total period of 20 minutes. A body with uniform motion has no acceleration. When the velocity of an object changes by the same amount each second or minute, you have uniform acceleration. Uniform deceleration is obtained when the decrease in velocity is the same each second or minute.

D. ENERGY

Energy may be described as the ability to do work. In the physical sense, work is done when a force acts on matter and moves it. We use heat energy to turn a steam turbine, and electric energy to drive motors. The mechanical energy of the pistons in an automobile engine is transmitted to the wheels by the crank shaft, transmission, drive shaft, differential gears, and rear axles. Nuclear energy is used to generate electric power and to drive naval ships.

Perhaps the most common definition of energy is given as "the capacity for doing work." However this is not quite a complete statement because energy can produce other effects which could not be considered as work. For example, heat can flow from one object to another without doing any work; yet heat is a form of energy and the process of heat transfer produces an effect. Therefore, a better definition of energy states that energy is the capacity for producing an effect.

Energy is normally classified according to the size and nature of the objects or particles with which it is associated. So we say that mechanical energy is the energy associated with large objectsusually things that are big enough to seesuch as pumps and turbines. Thermal energy is energy associated with molecules. Chemical energy is energy that arises from the forces which bind the atoms together in a molecule. Chemical energy is released whenever combustion or any other chemical reaction takes place. Electrical energy, light waves, and radio waves are examples of energy that are associated with particles smaller than atoms. Nuclear energy is obtained from splitting the atoms. Each of these types of energy (mechanical, thermal, etc.) must also be classified as either (1) stored energy, or (2) energy in transition.

Stored energy is thought of as energy that is actually contained in or stored in an object. There are two kinds of stored energy: potential energy and kinetic energy. Potential energy is energy in an object waiting to be released; while kinetic energy is energy that has been released. For example, potential energy exists in a rock resting on the edge of a cliff, water behind a dam, or steam behind a turbine throttle valve.

Kinetic energy exists because of the velocities of two or more objects. If you push the rock, open the gate of the dam, or open the turbine throttle valve, something will move. The rock will fall, the water will flow, and the steam will jet through the turbine nozzle valves. Thus the potential energy is converted to kinetic energy.

Energy in transition exists when the rock hits the ground, the water hits the bottom of the dam or the paddles of a water wheel, or when the steam hits the blades of the turbine rotor.

In the examples just discussed, an external source of energy was used to get things started. External energy was used to push the rock, open the gate of the dam, or to open the throttle valve. Thus you can see that one energy system affects another energy system. There is a tremendous amount of chemical energy stored in fuel oil; but it will not raise the steam in the boiler until some external energy has been expended to start the oil burning.

Energy can be measured. The most common measurement of expended energy is in work units of foot-pounds. When an object has been moved through a resisting force, work has been done.

E. WORK

The turbines and other power equipment used aboard ship are important because they do work. WORK is defined as the result of force moving through distance. The unit of measure for work is the FOOT-POUND (ft-lb).

The two parts of this unit are the POUND OF FORCE and the FOOT OF DISTANCE.

Force is measured in pounds. The gravitational pull on an object weighing 1 pound is a force of 1 pound. If you lift a 1-pound weight from ground level to a height of 1 foot, you exert a force of 1 pound through a distance of 1 foot and 1 foot-pound of work is done in the process. A force of 100 pounds is required to raise a 100-pound anvil; if you lift it to the top of a 30-inch bench, the work done is 2 1/2 ft x 100lb = 250 ft-lb. Work (in foot-pounds), therefore, equals the force (in pounds) times the distance (in feet).

Now suppose you want to move the anvil across the deck without lifting it. It will take a considerable force to slide the anvil—let us say 60 pounds. If you slide it 10 feet, you do 600 foot-pounds of work. Here the force of 60 pounds is required to overcome the resisting force of friction between the anvil and the deck. A great deal of the work done by any machine is the overcoming of the many frictional forces which resist the motion of the parts.

F. POWER

The ship's main engines are frequently called the POWER PLANT; and they are commonly rated according to how much power they can develop. For example, it might take one man 10 hours to load 20,000 pounds of ammunition on a truck, whereas a crane could do the same job in 5 minutes. The amount of work done is the same, but the crane is much more powerful than the man. It can do the work faster. POWER, then, relates to work and time. It is the TIME RATE of doing WORK. If we assume that the ammunition is raised an average height of 6 feet, the work done is equal to 6 ft x 20,000 lb or 120,000 ft-lb. Considering the man also as a machine, the power of each of the two machines is found by dividing this amount of work by the time required in each case. Expressing 10 hours in minutes, the man would work at the rate of 120,000 ft-lb ÷ 600 min = 200 ft-lb per min. The computed power of the crane would be 120,000 ft-lb ÷ 5 min = 24,000 ft-lb per min or 400 ft-lb per sec.

The most common unit of power is known as the HORSEPOWER. One horsepower is equivalent to 550 ft-lb per second, or 33,000 ft-lb per minute. Thus, if a lifting machine raises a weight of 100 pounds at the rate of 250 ft-lb per second, the machine is exerting only 0.454 of a horsepower (250 ft-lb ÷ 550 ft-lb = 0.454 hp).

If a crane hoists 2,000 pounds of cargo to a height of 30 feet in 5 seconds, how much horsepower is developed? Here is how to get the answer:

$$\text{Power} = \frac{\text{work}}{\text{time}} = \frac{2{,}000 \text{ lb} \times 30 \text{ ft}}{5 \text{ sec}}$$

$$= 12{,}000 \text{ ft-lb per sec}$$

$$\text{Horsepower} = \frac{12{,}000 \text{ ft-lb per sec}}{550 \text{ ft-lb per sec}} = 21.8$$

Or suppose a turbine has a known horsepower of 37,500 at rated capacity, and you want to know how much work it does. You find out by multiplying the developed horsepower by the hours in operation. This gives HORSEPOWER-HOURS, which is a measure of work for main propulsion machinery.

G. LAWS OF GASES

The energy transformation of major interest in the shipboard engineering plant is the transformation from heat to work. To see how this transformation occurs, we need to consider the pressure, temperature, and volume relationships which hold true for gases. In the middle of the 17th century, an English scientist, Robert Boyle, made some interesting discoveries concerning the relationship between the pressure, the temperature, and the volume of gases. In 1787, Jacques Charles, a Frenchman, proved that all gases expand the same amount when heated one degree if the pressure is kept constant. The relationships that these two men discovered are : summarized as follows:

1. When the temperature is held constant, increasing the pressure on a gas causes a pro- portional decrease in volume. Decreasing the pressure causes a proportional increase in volume.

2. When the pressure is held constant, increasing the temperature of a gas causes a proportional increase in volume. Decreasing the temperature causes a proportional decrease in volume.

3. When the volume is held constant, increasing the temperature of a gas causes a proportional increase in pressure. Decreasing the temperature causes a proportional decrease in pressure.

Suppose we have a boiler in which steam has just begun to form. With the steam stop valves still closed, the volume of the steam remains constant while the pressure and the temperature are both increasing. When operating pressure is reached, and the steam stop valves are opened, the high pressure of the steam causes the steam to flow to the turbines. The pressure of the steam thus provides the potential for doing work; the actual conversion of heat to work is done in the turbines.

H . PRESSURE AND VACUUM

Because pressure is very important to the engineering plant, it is necessary that you understand the relationships between gage pressure, atmospheric pressure, vacuum, and absolute pressure. These relationships are indicated in figure 3-1.

I .Gage Pressure

Gage pressure is the pressure actually shown on the dial of a gage which registers pressures at or above atmospheric pressure. Gage pressure is usually shown in pounds per square inch (psi); but it may be shown in inches of water, mercury, or other liquid. A reading of 1 inch of water means that the exerted pressure is able to support a column of water 1 inch high, or that a column of water in a U-tube would be displaced 1 inch by the pressure being measured. Similarly, a gage pressure reading of 12 inches of mercury means that the measured pressure is able to support a column of mercury 12 inches high. Gages are calibrated in inches of water

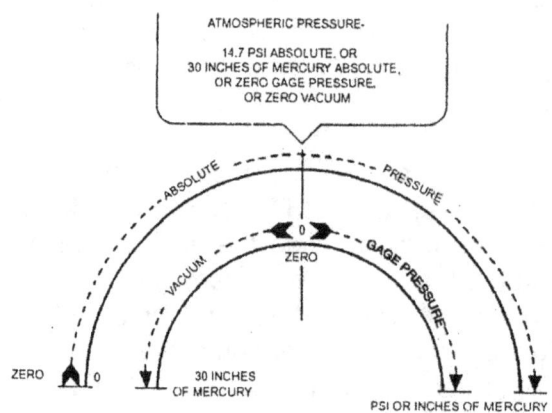

Figure 3-1.—Relationships between vacuum, gage pressure, absolute pressure, and atmospheric pressure.

when they are to be used for the measurement of very low pressures. Inches of mercury may be used when the range of pressures to be measured is somewhat higher, since mercury is about 14 times as heavy as water.

Note that a gage pressure reading of zero means that the pressure being measured is exactly the same as the existing atmospheric pressure. A gage reading of 50 psi means that the pressure being measured is 50 psi IN EXCESS OF the existing atmospheric pressure.

J. Atmospheric Pressure

Atmospheric pressure, or the pressure exerted by the weight of the air in the atmosphere, is measured with a BAROMETER (fig. 3-2). A barometer is similar to a manometer (see chapter 9), except that the indicating tube is sealed at the top. A barometer may be made by filling a tube with mercury and then inverting it so that the open end rests in a container of mercury which is open to the atmosphere. The absence of pressure at the closed end of the tube permits atmospheric pressure, acting upon the surface of the mercury in the open container, to hold the mercury in the tube at a height which corresponds to the pressure being exerted.

Normally, at sea level, atmospheric pressure will hold the column of mercury at a height of approximately 30 inches. Since a column of mercury 1 inch high exerts a pressure of 0.49 pounds per square inch, a 30-inch column of mercury exerts a pressure which is equal to (30 x 0.49) 14.7 pounds per square inch. Thus we can say that atmospheric pressure (zero gage pressure) at sea level is 14.7 psi, or 14.7 pounds per square inch absolute (psia). Notice, however, that this figure of 14.7 psi is the STANDARD for atmospheric pressure. Since fluctuations from this standard are shown on the barometer, the term BAROMETRIC PRESSURE is used to describe the atmospheric pressure which exists at any given moment. As a rule, you can use the term ATMOSPHERIC PRESSURE and the value 14.7 psi in place of the actual barometric pressure; but there may be times when it will be important to know the ACTUAL (barometric) pressure, in order to make precise measurements of gage pressure or vacuum.

K. Vacuum

A space in which the pressure is LESS than atmospheric pressure is said to be under VACUUM. The amount of vacuum is expressed in terms of the difference between the pressure in the space and the existing atmospheric pressure. Vacuum is measured in inches of mercury that is, the number of inches a column of mercury in a U-tube would be displaced by a pressure equal to the DIFFERENCE between the pressure in the vacuum space and the existing atmospheric pressure.

Vacuum gage scales are marked from 0 to 30. When a vacuum gage reads zero, the pressure in the space is the same as the existing atmospheric pressure or, in other words, there is no vacuum. A vacuum gage reading of 30 inches of mercury would indicate a nearly perfect vacuum. In actual practice, it is impossible to obtain a perfect vacuum; and the highest vacuum gage readings are seldom over 29 inches of mercury.

L. Absolute Pressure

Absolute pressure is atmospheric pressure PLUS gage pressure, or atmospheric pressure MINUS vacuum. For example, if gage pressure is 300 psi, absolute pressure is 314.7 psi; or if the measured vacuum is 10 inches of mercury, absolute pressure is approximately 20 inches of mercury. It is important to note that the amount of PRESSURE in a space under vacuum can be expressed only in terms of absolute pressure.

Sometimes it is necessary to convert a reading from inches of mercury to pounds per square inch. Figure 3-1 gives you all the information you need to make this conversion. Since atmospheric pressure is equal to 14.7 psi or to 30 inches of mercury, it is easy to see that 1 inch of mercury is equal to (14.7 psi divided by 30) 0.49 psi. Now convert your gage reading to absolute pressure (in inches of mercury) and then multiply this figure by 0.49 psi. For example, to convert a vacuum gage reading of 14 inches of mercury to psi, you would proceed as follows:

1. Convert 14 inches of mercury VACUUM to ABSOLUTE PRESSURE. Absolute pressure is atmospheric pressure MINUS vacuum (30 inches -14 inches = 16 inches).

2. Multiply the absolute pressure in inches of mercury by 0.49. Since 1 inch of mercury is equal to 0.49 psi, 16 inches of mercury is equal to (16 x 0.49 psi) 7.8 psi (about 8 psi). Remember that this answer is in terms of ABSOLUTE PRESSURE.

As you can see, it is also easy to convert psi to inches of mercury. Since atmospheric pressure is equal to 14.7 psi OR to 30 inches of mercury, 1 psi is equal to (30 inches of mercury divided by 14.7) 2.04 inches of mercury. For example, 10 psi absolute is equal to (10 x 2.04 inches of mercury) 20.4 inches of mercury absolute.

being measured PLUS the pressure exerted by the weight of the column of liquid above the gage. The required correction should be made in calibration of the gage; but if it has not been made in calibration, it must be made in the interpretation of the gage reading.

Correction for a head of liquid should be made as follows:

1. Measure the vertical distance from the center of the gage to the line in which the pressure is being measured.

2. For each foot of the distance measured, subtract from the gage reading the weight of a column of liquid 1 foot high and 1 inch square in cross section. If you are measuring pressure on a steam or water line, you must correct for a head of water. Since a column of water 1 foot high and 1 inch square in cross section weighs 0.433 pounds, you subtract 0.433 psi from the gage reading for each foot of drop. (CAUTION: The weight of each liquid is different, and must be determined before you can make this correction.)

For example, to correct a pressure gage reading for a head of water, assume that a steam pressure gage is connected 10 feet BELOW the steam line. The steam cools and condenses in the gage connection line, filling the connection line with water. The uncorrected gage reading is 250 psi. Multiply 0.433 psi by 10, and then subtract the resulting figure from 250 psi;

(1) 0.433 psi x 10 = 4.33 psi
(2) 250 psi - 4.33 psi - 245.67 psi

Thus the true pressure in the steam line is 245.67, or approximately 246 psi.

It is sometimes necessary to connect a water pressure gage at some distance ABOVE the point at which the pressure is being measured; then the reading on the gage will show the pressure being measured MINUS the pressure required to support the column of water up to the gage. To correct the reading, you must ADD the weight of the column of water-

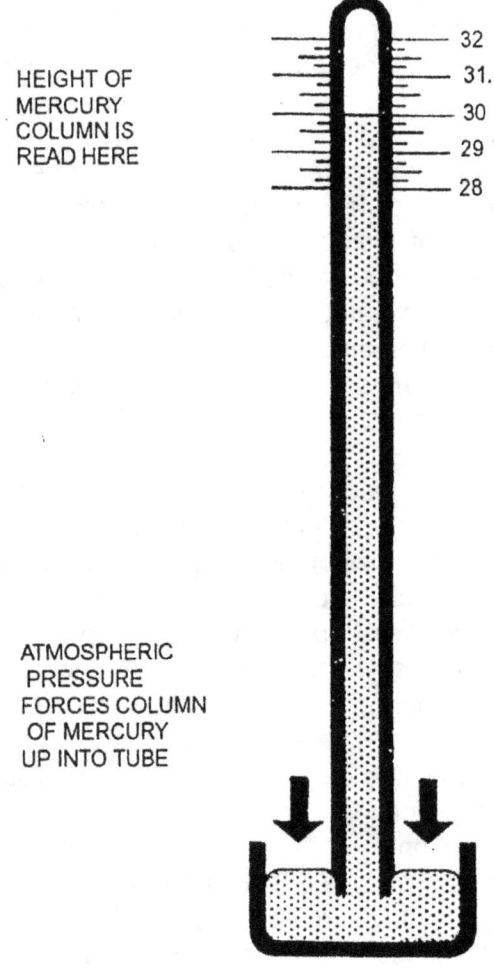

Figure 3-2.—Operating principle of mercurial barometer.

In order to interpret the reading on a pressure gage, you must know the LOCATION of the gage in relation to the line in which the pressure is being measured. As a general rule, pressure gage connections are led from the top of the pressure line. Occasionally, however, it is necessary to locate a pressure gage at some distance BELOW the pipe; then the reading on the gage will indicate the pressure that is, you must add 0.433 psi to the gage reading for each foot of rise.

For example, assume that a water pressure gage is connected 5 feet ABOVE the point at which the pressure is being measured. The gage reading is 30 psi. To obtain the actual pressure at the point of measurement, you must add (5 x 0.433 psi) 2.17 psi to the gage reading. Thus the actual pressure is 32.17 psi.

II. PRINCIPLES OF HYDRAULICS

The word hydraulics is derived from the Greek word for water (<u>hydor</u>) plus the Greek word for flute (<u>aulos</u>). The term "hydraulics" originally covered a study of the physical behavior of water at rest and in motion. However, the meaning of the term "hydraulics" has been broadened to cover the physical behavior of all liquids, including the oils that are used in present day hydraulic systems.

During the period before World War I, the Navy began to apply hydraulics extensively to naval mechanisms. Since that time, naval applications have increased to the point where many ingenious hydraulic devices are used in the solution of problems of gunnery, navigation, and aeronautics. Aboard ship today the applications of hydraulics include anchor windlasses, power cranes, steering gear, remote controls, power drives for the elevating of guns and training of mounts and turrets, powder and projectile hoists, recoil systems, gun rammers, and airplane catapults.

The foundations of modern hydraulics began in 1653 when Pascal discovered that "pressure set up in a liquid acts equally in all directions." This pressure acts at right angles to the containing surfaces.

In figure 3-3 if the liquid standing on a square inch (A) at the bottom of the tank weighs 8 pounds, a pressure of 8 pounds is exerted in every direction at A. The liquid resting on A will push equally downward and outward. But the liquid on every other square inch of the bottom surface is also pushing downward and outward in the same manner.

When we apply a force to the end of a column of confined liquid, the force is transmitted not only straight through to the other end, but also equally in every direction throughout the column-forwards, backwards, and sidewaysso that the containing vessel is literally filled with pressure. This is the reason that aflat fire hose takes on a circular cross-section when it is filled with water under pressure. The outward push of the water is equal in every direction. Water will leave the hose at the same velocity, through leaks, regardless of where the leaks are in the hose.

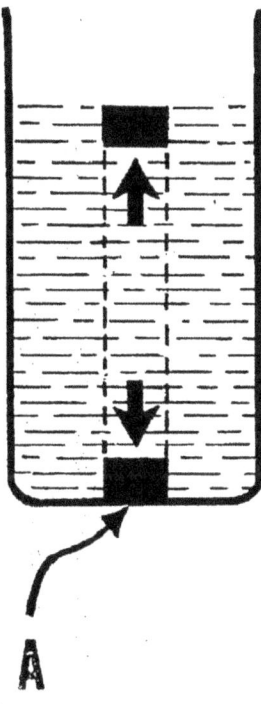

Figure 3-3.—Illustration showing principle of Pascal's law.

Let us now consider the effect of Pascal's law in the system shown in figure 3-4. If the force at piston A is 100 pounds and the area of the piston is 10 square inches, then the pressure in the liquid must be 10 pounds per square inch (psi). This pressure is transmitted to piston Bso that for every square inch of its area, piston B will be pushed upward with a force of 10 pounds. In this example we are merely considering a liquid column of equal cross-section so that the areas of the pistons are equal. All we have done is to carry a 100-poundforce around a bend; however, the principle illustrated is the basis for practically all mechanical hydraulics.

The same principle may be applied where the input piston is much smaller than the output piston or vice versa. Assume that the area of the input piston is 2 square inches and the area of the output piston is 20 square inches. If you apply a pressure of 20 pounds to the smaller piston, the pressure created in the liquid will again be 10 pounds per square inch because the force is concentrated on a smaller area. The upward force on the larger piston will be 200 pounds10 pounds for each of its 20 square inches. Thus you can see if two pistons are used in a hydraulic system, the force acting on each piston will be directly proportional to its area, and the magnitude of each force will be the product of the pressure and the area of the piston.

III. PRINCIPLES OF PNEUMATICS

Pneumatics is that branch of mechanics that deals with the mechanical properties of gases. Perhaps the most common application of these properties is the use of compressed air. Compressed air is used to transmit pressure, according to Pascal's principle, in a variety of applications. For example, in tires and air cushioned springs, compressed air acts as a cushion to absorb shock. Air brakes on locomotives and large trucks contribute greatly to the safety of railroad and truck transportation. Compressed air is used in numerous ways. For example, tools such as riveting hammers and pneumatic drills are air operated. Automatic combustion control systems utilize compressed air for the operation of the instruments. Compressed air is also used in diving bells and diving suits. Perhaps a brief discussion on the use of compressed air as an aid in the control of submarines will best explain the theory of pneumatics.

Submarines are designed with a number of tanks that may be used for the control of the ship. These tanks may be flooded with water to submerge; or they may be filled with compressed air to surface.

The compressed air for the pneumatic system is maintained in storage tanks (called banks) at a pressure of 4,500 psi. When surfacing, the pneumatic system delivers compressed air to the desired control tanks. Since the pressure of the air is greater than the pressure of the water, the water is forced out of the tank. As a result, the weight of the ship is decreased; it becomes more buoyant, and thus it will tend to rise to the surface.

A. HEAT

You undoubtedly know from experience that heat and temperature are related; however, they are not the same. Water from a water main feels cool until it has been over a fire a few minutes. It evidently must have received something from the fire. If you place two pennies together, one of which was heated by being held in the flame of a match, in a short time the two pennies will be equally warm. Again something passed into the cooler object and made it hot. That something is called heat.

Many forms of mechanical action also produce considerable quantities of heat. For example, you rub your hands together to warm them when they are cold. Matches are ignited by rubbing them on a rough surface. A Shipfitter can notice heat in a piece of metal after hammering it; and the head of a nail is heated when the nail is driven into wood.

The molecules in the nail (as in all matter) are in continual motion. The blow on the nail increases the molecular motion. The molecules in the top layer receive the impulse from the hammer, and vibrate with greater violence. The increased vibration and energy of motion is passed on to layer after layer of molecules. Thus the effect of the blow is to produce ageneral increase in the motion of the molecules. This energy of molecular motion is called heat.

Because molecules are constantly in motion, they exert a pressure on the walls of the pipe, boiler, cylinder, or other object in which they are contained. Also, the temperature of any substance arises from and is directly proportional to the activity of the molecules. Therefore, every time you read thermometers and pressure gages you are finding out something about the amount of internal energy contained in the substance. High pressures and temperatures indicate that the molecules are moving rapidly and that the substance therefore has a lot of internal energy.

HEAT is a more familiar term than internal energy, yet one that may actually be more difficult to define correctly. The important thing to remember is that heat is THERMAL ENERGY IN TRANSITION—that is, it is thermal energy that is moving from one substance or system to another.

An example will help to illustrate the difference between heat and internal energy. Suppose there are two equal lengths of pipe, made of identical materials and containing steam at the same pressure and temperature. One pipe is well insulated, the other is not insulated at all. From everyday experience you know that more heat will flow from the uninsulated pipe than from the insulated pipe. When the two pipes are first filled with steam, the steam in one pipe contains exactly as much internal energy as the steam in the other pipe. We know this is true because the two pipes contain equal volumes of steam at the same pressure and at the same temperature. After a few minutes, the steam in the uninsulated pipe will contain much less internal energy than the steam in the insulated pipe, as we can tell by measuring the pressure and the temperature of the steam in each pipe. What has happened ? Stored thermal energy—internal energy—has moved from one place to another, first from the steam to the pipe, then from the uninsulated pipe to the air. The MOVEMENT or FLOW of thermal energy is what should be called heat.

B. Units of Measurement

Both internal energy and heat are usually measured using the unit called the BRITISH THERMAL UNIT (Btu). For most practical engineering purposes, 1 Btu is defined as the amount of thermal energy required to raise the temperature of 1 pound of water through 1°F.

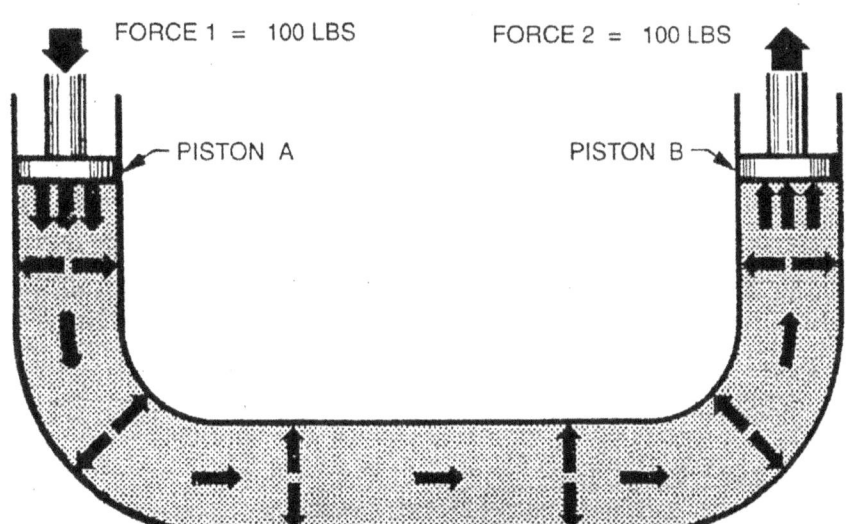

Figure 3-4.—Principle of mechanical hydraulics.

When large amounts of thermal energy are involved, it is usually more convenient to use multiples of the Btu. For example, 1 kB is equal to 1,000 Btu, and 1 mB is equal to 1,000,000 Btu.

Another unit in which thermal energy may be measured is the CALORIE, the amount of heat required to raise the temperature of 1 gram of water 1°C. One Btu equals 252 calories.

C. Sensible Heat and Latent Heat

The terms SENSIBLE HEAT and LATENT HEAT are often used to indicate the effect that the flow of heat has on a substance. The flow of heat from one substance to another is normally reflected in a temperature change in each substance—the hotter substance becomes cooler, the cooler substance becomes hotter. However, the flow of heat is NOT reflected in a temperature change in a substance which is in the process of changing from one physical state (solid, liquid, or gas) to another. When the flow of heat is reflected in a temperature change, we say that SENSIBLE HEAT has been added to or removed from the substance. When the flow of heat is NOT reflected in a temperature change but IS reflected in the changing physical state of s substance, we say that LATENT HEAT has been added or removed.

Does anything bother you in this last paragraph? It should. Here we are, talking about adding and removing heat. And, furthermore, we are talking about sensible heat and latent heat as though we had two different kinds of heat to consider. As noted before, this is common (if inaccurate) engineering language. So keep the following points clearly in mind: (1) heat is the flow of thermal energy; (2) when we talk about adding and removing heat, we mean that we are providing temperature differentials so that thermal energy can flow from one substance to another; and (3) when we talk about sensible heat and latent heat, we are talking about two different kinds of EFFECTS that can be produced by heat, but not about two different kinds of heat.

The three basic physical states of all matter are SOLID, LIQUID, and GAS (or vapor). The physical state of a substance is closely related to the distance between molecules. As a general rule, the molecules are closest together in solids, farther apart in liquids, and farthest apart in gases. When the flow of heat to a substance is not reflected in a temperature change, we know that the energy is being used to increase the distance between the molecules of the substance and thus to change it from a solid to a liquid or from a liquid to a gas. You might say that latent heat is the energy price that must be paid for a change of state from solid to liquid or from liquid to gas. The energy is not lost; rather, it is stored in the substance as internal energy. The energy price is "repaid," so to speak, when the substance changes back from gas to liquid or from liquid to solid, since heat flows FROM the substance during these changes of state.

Figure 3-5 shows the relationship between sensible heat and latent heat for one substance, water, at atmospheric pressure. (The same kind of chart could be drawn up for other substances; however, different amounts of thermal energy would be involved in the changes of state.)

If we start with 1 pound of ice at 0° F, we must add 16 Btu in order to raise the temperature of the ice to 32° F. We call this adding SENSIBLE HEAT. To change the pound of ice at 32° F to a pound of water at 32°F, we must add 144 Btu (the LATENT HEAT OF FUSION). There will be no change in temperature while the ice is melting. After all the ice has melted, however, the temperature of the water will be raised as additional heat is supplied. If we add 180 Btu that is, 1 Btu for each degree of temperature between 32° F and 212 F the temperature of the water, will be raised to the boiling point. To change the pound of water at 212° F to a pound of steam at 212° F, we must add 970 Btu (the LATENT HEAT OF VAPORIZA-

TION). After all the water has been converted to steam, the addition of more heat will cause an increase in the temperature of the steam. If we add about 44 Btu to the pound of steam which is at 210° F, we can superheat it to 300° F.

The same relationships apply when heat is being removed. The removal of 44 Btu from the pound of steam which is at 300° F will cause the temperature to drop to 212° F. As the pound of steam at 212° F changes to a pound of water at 212° F, 970 Btu are given off. When a substance is changing from a gas or vapor to a liquid, we usually use the term LATENT HEAT OF CONDENSATION for the heat that is given off. Notice, however, that the latent heat of condensation is exactly the same as the latent heat of vaporization. The removal of another 180 Btu of sensible heat will lower the temperature of the pound of water from 212° F to 32° F. As the pound of water at 32° F changes to a pound of ice at 32° F, 144 Btu are given off without any accompanying change in temperature. Further removal of heat causes the temperature of the ice to decrease.

D. TEMPERATURE

The temperature of an object is a measure of how hot or cold the object is; and it can be measured by thermometers and read on their temperature scales.

The TEMPERATURE SCALES employed to measure temperature are the Fahrenheit scale and the centigrade scale. In engineering and for practically all purposes in the Navy, the Fahrenheit scale is used. It may, however, be necessary for you to convert centigrade readings to the Fahrenheit scale, so both scales are explained here.

The FAHRENHEIT SCALE has two main reference points the boiling point of pure water at 212, and the freezing point of pure water at 32. The size of the Fahrenheit degree is 1/180 of the total temperature change from 32 to 212. And the scale can be extended in either directionto higher temperatures without any limits, and (by using MINUS degrees) to lower temperatures down to the lowest temperature theoretically possible, the so-called ABSOLUTE ZERO. This temperature is -460, or 492 below the freezing point of water.

In the CENTIGRADE SCALE, the freezingpoint of pure water is 0 and the boiling point of pure water is 100. Therefore, 0° C and 100° C are equivalent to 32° F and 212° F, respectively. Each centigrade degree is larger than a Fahrenheit degree (since there are only 100 centigrade degrees between the freezing and boiling points of water, while this same temperature change requires 180 degrees in the, Fahrenheit scale). Therefore the centigrade degree is 180/100 or 1.8 Fahrenheit degrees. In the centigrade scale absolute zero is -273.

Figure 3-6 shows the two temperature scales in comparison. This figure also introduces the simplest of the temperature measuring instruments, the liquid-in-glass THERMOMETER. The two thermometers shown are exactly alike in SIZE and SHAPE, the only difference being in the outside markings or SCALES on them. Each thermometer is a hollow glass tube which has a mercury-filled bulb at the bottom, and which is sealed at the top. Mercury, like any liquid, expands on being heated, and it will rise in the hollow tube. The illustration shows the Fahrenheit thermometer with its bulb standing in ice water (32° F), while the centigrade thermometer is in boiling water (100° C).

The essential point to remember is that the level of the mercury in a thermometer depends only on the temperature to which the bulb is exposed. If you were to exchange the thermometers, the mercury in the centigrade thermometer would drop to the level at which the mercury now stands in the Fahrenheit thermometer, while the mercury in the Fahrenheit thermometer would rise to the level at which the mercury now stands in the centigrade

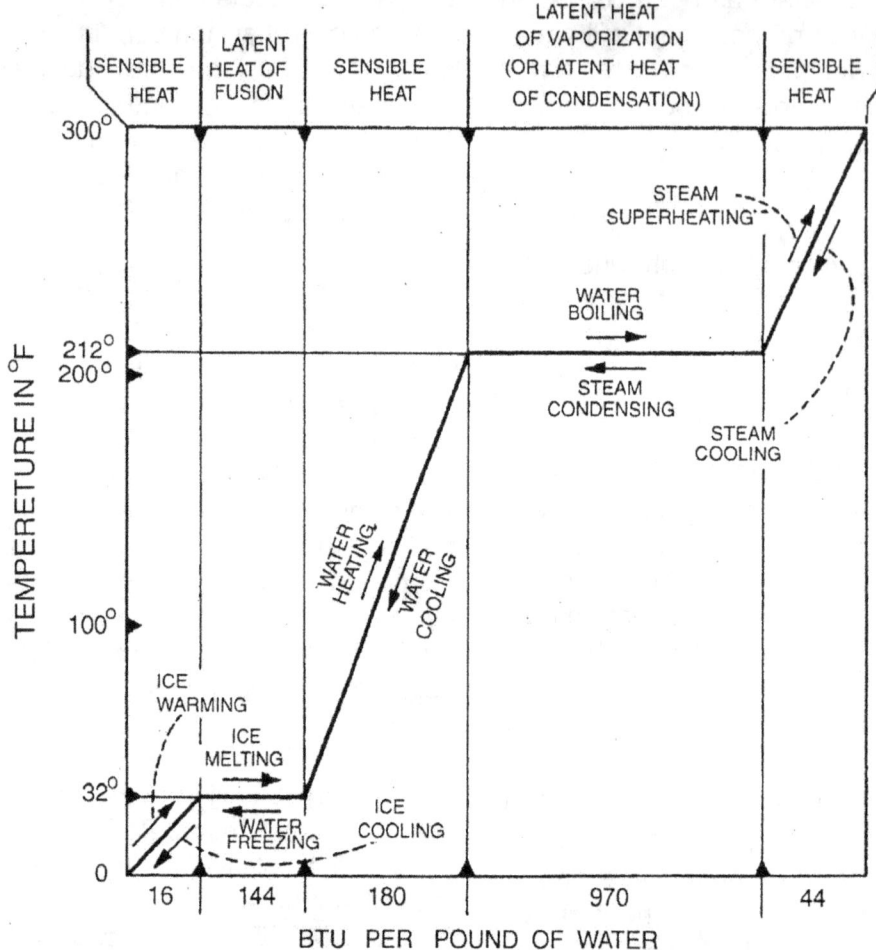

Figure 3-5.—Relationship between sensible heat and latent heat for water at atmospheric pressure.

thermometer. The temperatures would be 0° C for the ice water and 212° F for the boiling water.

If you place both thermometers in water containing lumps of ice, the Fahrenheit thermometer will read 32 and the centigrade thermometer will read 0. Heat the water slowly. The temperature will not change until the ice in the water has completely melted (a great deal of heat is required just to melt the ice), then both mercury columns will begin to rise. When the mercury level is at the +10 mark in the centigrade thermometer, it will be at the +50 mark in the Fahrenheit thermometer. The two columns will rise together at the same speed, and when the water finally boils they will stand at 100° C and 212° F, respectively. The same temperature change that is, the same amount of heat transferred to the waterhas raised the temperature 100 entigrade degrees and 180 Fahrenheit degrees, but the actual change in heat energy is EXACTLY THE SAME.

E. COMBUSTION

The term "combustion" refers to the rapid chemical union of oxygen with the fuel. The perfect combustion of fuel should result in carbon dioxide, nitrogen, water vapor, and sulphur dioxide. The oxygen furnished to the fuel, in order to burn it, is obtained from the air. Air is a mechanical mixture containing by weight 23.15 percent oxygen and 76.85 percent nitrogen. The oxygen only is used in combustion of the fuel; the nitrogen, being an inert gas, has no chemical effect upon the combustion.

The chemical combination obtained during combustion results in the liberation of heat energy, a portion of which is used to propel the ship. Actually, what happens is a rearrangement of the atoms of the chemical elements into new combinations of molecules. In other words, as the temperature of the fuel oil in the presence of oxygen is increased to the ignition point, the various chemical elements in the fuel begin to separate from each other and unite with certain amounts of oxygen, to form entirely new substances, which give off heat energy in the process. A good fuel has a high speed of combustion, thus producing a large amount of heat in a short time.

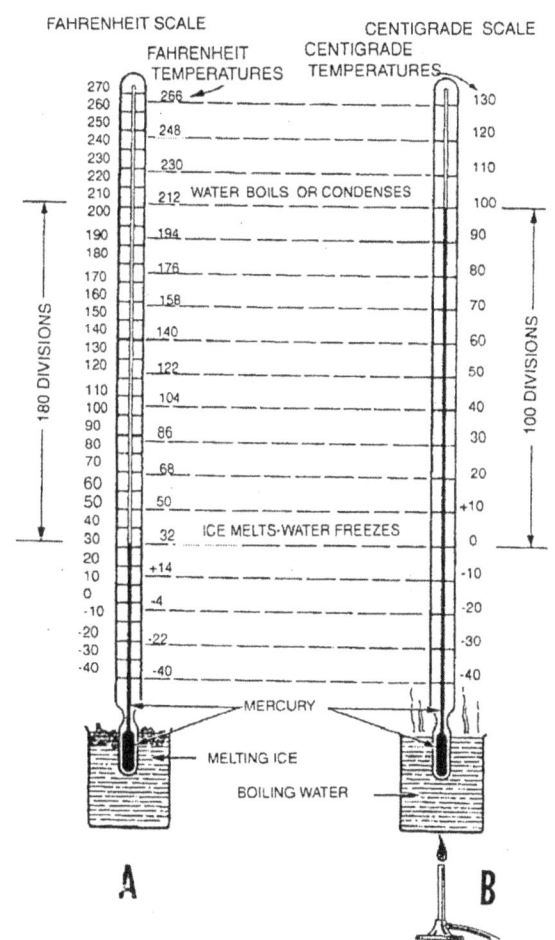

Figure 3-6.—Temperature scales: A. Fahrenheit p. scale. B. Centigrade scale.

PERFECT COMBUSTION cannot as yet be achieved in either a boiler or the cylinders of an internal combustion engine, but this is the objective. Theoretically, it is simple. It consists of bringing each particle of the fuel (heated to its ignition temperature) into contact with the correct amount of oxygen. The following factors are involved:

1. Sufficient air must be supplied.

2. The air and fuel particles must be thoroughly mixed.

3. Temperatures must be high enough to maintain combustion.

4. Enough time must be allowed to permit completion of the process.

What is known as COMPLETE COMBUSTION, however, can be achieved. This is accomplished by supplying more oxygen to the process than would be required if perfect combustion were possible. The result is that some of the excess oxygen appears in the combustion gases.

F. STEAM

Steam is water to which enough heat has been added to convert it from the liquid to the gaseous state. When heat is added to water in an open container, steam forms, but it quickly mixes with air and cools back to water that is dispersed in the air, making the air more humid. If you add the heat to water in a closed container, the steam builds up pressure. If you add exactly enough heat to convert all the water to steam at the temperature of boiling water, you get saturated steam. SATURATED STEAM is steam saturated with all the heat it can hold at the boiling temperature of water.

The boiling temperature of water becomes higher as the pressure over the water becomes higher. Steam hotter than the boiling temperature of water is called SUPERHEATED STEAM. When steam has 250° F of superheat, the actual temperature is the boiling temperature plus 250° F. At 600 psi the boiling temperature of water is 489° F. So if steam at 600 psi has 250° F of superheat, its actual temperature is 739° F. WET STEAM is steam at the boiling temperature, but still containing some water particles. DESUPERHEATED STEAM is steam which has been cooled by being passed through a pipe extending through the steam drum; in the process the steam loses all but about 20 or 30 of its superheat. The advantage of desuperheated steam is that it is certain to be dry, and yet it is not so hot that special alloy steels would be required for the construction of the piping that carries the desuperheated steam.

IV. METALS

As you look around, you can see that not only is a ship constructed of metal, but that the boilers, piping system, machinery, and even a bunk and locker are constructed of some type of metal. No one type of metal can serve all the needs aboard ship, so many types of metals or metal alloys must be used. For some parts of a ship a strong metal must be used and on other parts a lightweight metal is needed. Some areas require special metal that can be shaped or worked very easily.

The physical properties of some metals or metal alloys make them more suitable for one use than for another. Various terms are used in describing the physical properties of metals. By studying the following explanations of these terms you should have a better understanding of why certain metals are used on one part of a ship's structure and not on another part.

STRENGTH refers to the ability of a metal to maintain heavy loads (or force) without breaking. Steel, for example, is strong, but lead is weak.

HARDNESS refers to the ability of a metal to resist penetration, wear, or cutting action.

MALLEABILITY is a property of a metal that allows it to be rolled, forged, hammered, or shaped, without cracking or breaking. Copper is a very malleable metal.

BRITTLENESS—any metal that will shatter easily is brittle. Metals such as cast iron or cast aluminum, and some very hard steels are brittle.

DUCTILITY refers to the ability of a metal to stretch or bend without breaking. Soft iron, soft steel, and copper are ductile metals.

TOUGHNESS-metal that will not tear or shear (cut) easily and that will stretch without breaking has the property of toughness.

Metal preservation aboard ship is a continuous operation since the metals are constantly exposed to fumes, water, acids, and moist salt air; all of these will eventually cause corrosion. The corrosion of iron and steel is called rusting and results in the formation of iron oxide (iron and oxygen) on the surface of the metal. Iron oxide (or rust) can be easily identified by its reddish color. (A blackish hue occurs in the first stage of rusting, but is seldom thought of as rust.) Corrosion can be reduced, or prevented, by using better grades of base metals, by adding special metals such as nickel and chromium, or by coating the surface with paint or other metal preservatives.

Metals and alloys are divided into two general classes; ferrous and nonferrous. Ferrous metals are those that are composed primarily of iron. Nonferrous metals are those that are composed primarily of some element or elements other than iron. One way to tell a common ferrous metal from a nonferrous metal, is by using a magnet; most ferrous metal is magnetic and non-ferrous metal is nonmagnetic.

To obtain the desired physical properties of a metal, elements must be alloyed (or mixed) together. For example, by alloying (or mixing) chromium and nickel with iron, a metal known as special treated steel is produced. Special treated steel (STS) has great resistance to penetrating and shearing forces and is used for gun shields, turrets, protective decks, and other vital areas. A nonferrous alloy that has many uses aboard ship is copper-nickel, which is used extensively in salt water piping systems. Copper-nickel is produced by mixing copper and nickel.

GLOSSARY OF ENGINEERING TERMS

TABLE OF CONTENTS

	Page
Automatic Bus Transfer ... Boiler Tube Cleaner	1
Boiler Water ... Distillate	2
Distilling Plants ... Forging	3
Fresh Water System ... Log Book	4
Log, Engineering ... Parts Per Million	5
Preheating ... Static	6
Steam Lance ... Wireways	7
Work Request ... Zinc	8

GLOSSARY OF ENGINEERING TERMS

ABT (AUTOMATIC BUS TRANSFER): An automatic electrical device that supplies power to vital equipment. This device will shift from the normal power supply to an alternate power supply when the normal supply is interrupted.

ACETYLENE: A gas that is chemically produced from calcium carbide and water, used for welding and cutting.

ADAPTER: A coupling or similar device that permits fittings with different-sized openings (apertures) to be joined together.

AIR EJECTOR: A type of jet pump, used to remove air and other gases from the condensers.

AIR CHAMBER: A chamber, usually bulb-shaped, on the suction and discharge sides of a pump. Air in the chamber acts as a cushon and prevents sudden shocks to the pump.

AIR REGISTER: A device in the casing of a boiler, used for regulating the amount of air for combustion and to provide a circular motion to the air.

AISE: Association of Iron and Steel Engineers.

ALLOY: A mixture composed of two or more metals.

ALTERNATING CURRENT (A-C): Current that is constantly changing in value and direction at regular recurring intervals.

AMBIENT TEMPERATURE: The temperature of the surrounding area.

AMMETER: An instrument for measuring the rate of flow of electrical current in amperes.

ANNEALING: The softening of metal by heating and slow cooling.

ANNUNCIATOR: See ENGINE ORDER TELEGRAPH.

ARGON: An inert gas, slightly heavier than air, used in inert-gas shielded metal arc welding.

ARMORED CABLE: An electric cable that is protected on the outside by a metal covering.

ASTM: American Society for Testing Metals.

AUTOMATIC COMBUSTION CONTROL SYSTEM (ACC): A system that provides a means of automatically controlling the fuel and air mixture in a boiler.

BACK PRESSURE: The pressure exerted on the exhaust side of a pump or engine.

BDC (BOTTOM DEAD CENTER): The position of a reciprocating piston at its lowest point of travel.

BALLASTING: The process of filling empty tanks with salt water, to protect the ship from underwater damage and increase its stability. See DEBALLASTING.

BLUEPRINTS: Reproduced copies of drawings (usually having white lines on a blue background.

BOILER: A strong' metal tank or vessel composed of tubes, drums, and headers, in which water is heated by the gases of combustion to form steam.

BOILER CENTRAL CONTROL STATION: A centrally located station for directing the control of all boilers in the fireroom.

BOILER DESIGN PRESSURE: Pressure specified by the manufacturer, usually about 103% of normal steam drum operating pressure.

BOILER INTERNAL FITTINGS: All parts inside the boiler which control the flow of steam and water.

BOILER OPERATING PRESSURE: The pressure required to be maintained in a boiler while in service.

BOILER OPERATING STATION: A location from which boilers are operated.

BOILER RECORD SHEET: A NavShips form maintained for each boiler, which serves as a monthly summary of operation.

BOILER REFRACTORIES: Materials used in the boiler furnace to protect the boiler from heat of combustion.

BOILER ROOM: A compartment containing boilers but not containing a station for operating or firing the boilers. Refers specifically to bulkhead enclosed boiler installations.

BOILER TUBE CLEANER: A CYLINDRICAL brush that is used to clean the insides of boiler tubes.

BOILER WATER: Refers to the water actually contained in the boiler.

BRAZING: A method of joining two metals at high temperature with a molten alloy.

BRINE: A highly concentrated solution of salt in water, normally associated with the overboard discharge of distilling plants.

BRITTLENESS: That property of a material which causes it to fracture prior to any noticeable signs of deformation.

BURNERMAN: Man in fireroom who tends the burners in the boilers.

BUSHING: A renewable lining for a hole through which a moving part passes.

BYPASS: To divert the flow of gas or liquid. Also, the line that diverts the flow.

CALIBRATION: The comparison of any measuring instrument with a set standard.

CANTILEVER: A projecting arm or beam supported only at one end.

CAPILLARY TUBE: A slender thin-walled small-bored tube used with remote-reading indicators.

CARBON DIOXIDE: A colorless, orderless gas used as a fire extinguishing agent and for inflating liferafts and lifejackets.

CARBON PACKING: Pressed segments of graphite used to prevent steam leakage around shafts.

CASUALTY POWER SYSTEM: A means of using portable cables to transmit power to vital equipment in an emergency.

CHECK VALVE: A valve that permits a flow of liquid in one direction only.

CHILL SHOCKING: A method of removing scale from the tubes of a distilling plant, utilizing steam and cold water.

CHLORINE: A heavy gas, greenish-yellow in color used for water purification, sewage disposal, and in the preparation of bleaching solutions. Poisonous in concentrated form.

CIRCUIT BREAKER: An electrical device that provides circuit overload protection.

CLUTCH: A form of coupling which is designed to connect or disconnect a driving or driven member.

COMPARTMENT CHECKOFF LIST: A list of all damage control fittings, their location, and status for different ship conditions.

CONDENSER: A heat transfer device in which steam or vapor is condensed to water.

CONDUCTION: A method of heat transfer from one body to another when the two bodies are in physical contact.

CONSTANT PRESSURE GOVERNOR: A device that maintains a constant pump discharge pressure under varying loads.

CONTROLLER: A device used to stop, start, and protect motors from overloads, while they are running.

CORROSION: The process of being eaten away gradually by chemical action, such as rusting.

COUNTERSINK: A cone-shaped tool used to enlarge and bevel one end of a drilled hole.

CROSS-CONNECTED PLANT: A method of operating two or more plants as one unit, having a common steam supply.

CURTIS STAGE: A velocity-compounded impulse turbine stage having one pressure drop in the nozzles and two velocity drops in the blading.

DEAERATING FEED TANK (DA TANK): A unit in the steam-water cycle used to (1) free the condensate of dissolved oxygen, (2) heat the feed water, and (3) act as a reservoir for feed water.

DEBALLASTING: The process of emptying salt from tanks, to protect the ship from underwater damage and increase its stability.

DEGREE OF SUPERHEAT: The amount by which the temperature of steam exceeds saturation temperature.

DIATOMACEOUS EARTH: A light, crumbly silica material derived from algae and microscopic skeletons. It has relatively high absorption and filtering qualities.

DIATOMITE FILTERS: Filters made of a diatomaceous earth and asbestos filler.

DIRECT CURRENT (D-C): Current that moves in one direction only.

DIRECT DRIVE: One in which the drive mechanism is coupled directly to the driven member.

DISTILLATE: Fresh water produced in distilling plants.

DISTILLING PLANTS: Units commonly called evaporators (evaps) used to convert seawater into fresh water.

DRAWING: The plans used to show the fabrication and assembly details.

DRUM, STEAM: The large tank at the top of the boiler in which the steam collects.

DRUM, WATER: A tank at the bottom of a boiler; also called MUD DRUM.

DRY PIPE: A perforated pipe at the highest point in a steam drum to collect steam.

DUCTILITY: Property possessed by metals that allows them to be drawn or stretched.

ECONOMIZER: A heat transfer device on a boiler that uses the gases of combustion to preheat the feed water.

EDUCTOR: A jet type pump (no moving parts) used to empty flooded spaces.

EFFICIENCY: The ratio of the output to the input.

ELASTICITY: The ability of a material to return to its original size and shape.

ELECTRODE: A metallic rod (welding rod) used in electric welding that melts when current is passed through it.

ELECTROHYDRAULIC STEERING: A system having a motor-driven hydraulic pump that creates the force needed to actuate the rams to position the ship's rudder.

ELECTROLYSIS: A chemical action that takes place between unlike metals in systems using salt water.

ELECTROMOTIVE FORCE (EMF): A force that causes electrons to move through a closed circuit; expressed in volts.

ELEMENT: A substance which consists of chemically united atoms of one kind.

ENERGY: The capacity for doing work.

ENGINEER'S BELL BOOK: A legal record maintained by the throttle watch of all ordered main engine speed changes.

ENGINE ORDER TELEGRAPH: A device on the ship's bridge to give orders to the engine-room. Also called ANNUNCIATOR.

EPM (EQUIVALENTS PER MILLION): The number of equivalent parts of a substance per million parts of another substance. The word "equivalent" refers to the equivalent weight of a substance.

EXPANSION JOINT: A junction which allows for expansion and contraction.

FATIGUE: The tendency of a material to break under repeated strain.

FEED HEATER: A heat transfer device used to heat the feed water before it goes to the boiler.

FEED WATER: Fresh water, with the highest possible level of purity, made in EVAPORATORS for use in boilers.

FERROUS METAL: Metal with a high iron content.

FIREBOX: The section of a ship's boiler where fuel oil combustion takes place.

FIREMAIN: The salt water line that provides fire-fighting and flushing water throughout the ship.

FIRE TUBE BOILER: Boilers in which the gases of combustion pass through the tubes and heat the water surrounding them.

FLAREBACK: A backfire of flame and hot gases into a ship's fireroom from the firebox. Caused by a fuel oil explosion in the firebox.

FLASH POINT OF OIL: That temperature at which the oil vapor will flash into fire but the main body of the oil will not ignite.

FLEXIBLE I-BEAM: An I-shaped steel beam on which the forward end of a turbine is mounted; it allows for longitudinal expansion and contraction.

FLOOR PLATES: The removable deck plating of a fireroom or engineroom aboard ship.

FLUX: A chemical agent that retards oxidation of the surface, removes oxides already present, and aids fusion.

FORCE: Anything that tends to produce or modify motion.

FORCED DRAFT: A term used to describe air under pressure supplied to the burners in a ship's boiler.

FORCED DRAFT BLOWERS: Turbine-driven fans which supply air to the boiler furnace.

FORCED FEED LUBRICATION: A lubrication system that uses a pump to maintain a constant pressure.

FORGING: The forming of metal by heating and hammering.

FRESH WATER SYSTEM: A piping system which supplies fresh water throughout the ship.

FUEL OIL MICROMETER VALVE: A valve installed at the burner manifold, which is used to control the fuel oil pressure to the burners.

FUEL OIL SERVICE TANKS: Tanks from which the fuel oil service pumps take suction for discharging oil to the burners.

FUSE: A protective device that is designed to open a circuit if the current flow exceeds a predetermined value.

GAGE GLASS: A device for indicating the liquid level in a tank.

GAS-FREE: A term used to describe a space that has been tested and found safe for hot work (welding & cutting).

GEARED-TURBINE DRIVE: A turbine that drives a pump, generator, or other machinery through reduction gears.

GROUNDED PLUG: A three pronged electrical plug used for grounding portable tools to the ship's structure. It is a safety device which always must be checked prior to using portable tools.

HAGEVAP SOLUTION: A chemical compound used in distilling plants, to prevent the formation of scale.

HALIDE LEAK DETECTOR: A device that is used to locate leaks in refrigeration systems.

HANDHOLE: An opening that is large enough for the hand and arm to enter the boiler for making slight repairs, and for inspection.

HANDY BILLY: A small portable water pump.

HARDENING: The heating and rapid cooling (quenching) of metal to induce hardness.

HARDNESS: The ability of a material to resist penetration.

HEAT EXCHANGER: Any device that is designed to allow the transfer of heat from one fluid (liquid or gas) to another.

HYDROGEN: A highly explosive, light, invisible, non-poisonous gas used for underwater welding and cutting operations.

HYDROMETER: An instrument used for determining the specific gravity of liquids.

HYDROSTATIC TEST: A pressure test using water to detect leaks in a boiler or other closed systems.

IGNITION, COMPRESSION: Ignition where the heat generated by compression in an internal combustion engine ignites the fuel (as in a diesel engine).

IGNITION, SPARK: Ignition where the mixture of air and fuel in an internal combustion-engine is ignited by an electric spark (as in a gasoline engine).

IMPELLER: An encased, rotating element provided with vanes which draw in fluid at the center and expel it at a high velocity at the outer edge.

IMPULSE TURBINE: A turbine in which the major part of the driving force is received from the impulse of incoming steam.

INDIRECT DRIVE: A drive mechanism coupled to the driven member by gears or belts.

INERT: Inactive.

INJECTOR: A device which, by means of a jet of steam, forces water into the boiler, or as in the diesel engineforces fuel into the cylinders.

INSULATION: A material used to retard heat transfer.

JACKBOX: Receptacle, usually secured to a bulkhead, in which telephone jacks are mounted.

JOB ORDER: The order issued by a repair activity to its own subdivisions, to perform a repair job in response to a WORK REQUEST.

JUMPER: Any connecting pipe, hose, or wire, normally for use in emergencies aboard ship, used to bypass damaged sections of a pipe, a hose, or & wire. (See BYPASS.)

JURY RIG: Any temporary or makeshift device.

LABYRINTH PACKING: Rows of metallic strips or fins used to prevent steam leakage along the shaft or a turbine.

LAGGING: A protective and confining cover placed over insulating material.

LIGHT OFF: Start, literally; 'to start a fire in," as in "light off a boiler."

LOG BOOK: Any chronological record of events, such as an engineering watch log.

LOG, ENGINEERING: A legal record of important events and data concerning the machinery of a ship.

LOG ROOM: Engineer's office on board ship.

LUBE OIL PURIFIER: A unit that removes water and sediment from lubricating oil by centrifugal force.

MACHINABILITY: The term used to describe the ease with which a metal may be turned, planed, milled, or otherwise shaped.

MAIN CONDENSER: A heat exchanger which converts exhaust steam to feed water.

MAIN DRAIN SYSTEM: The system used for pumping bilges, consisting of pumps and associated piping.

MAKEUP FEED: Water of required purity intended for use in ship's boilers. It is the water needed to replace that lost in the steam cycle.

MALLEABILITY: That property of a material which enables it to be stamped, hammered, or rolled into thin sheets.

MANIFOLD: A fitting with numerous branches used to convey fluids between a large pipe and several smaller pipes.

MECHANICAL ADVANTAGE (MA): The advantage (leverage) gained by the use of such devices as a wheel to open a large valve, chain falls and block and tackle to lift heavy weights, and wrenches to tighten nuts on bolts.

MECHANICAL CLEANING: A method of cleaning the firesides of boilers by scraping and wire-brushing.

MICROMHOS: Electrical units used with salinity indicators for measuring the conductivity of water.

MOTOR GENERATOR SET: A machine which consists of a motor mechanically coupled to a generator and usually mounted on the same base.

NAVY BOILER COMPOUND: A powdered chemical mixture used in boiler water treatment to convert scale-forming salts into sludge.

NAVY SPECIAL FUEL OIL (NSFO): The name applied to the grade of fuel oil that the Navy uses in combatant ships.

NIGHT ORDER BOOK: A notebook containing standing and special instructions by the engineer officer to the night engineering officer of the watch.

NITROGEN: An inert gas which will not support life or combustion. Used in recoil systems and other spaces requiring an inert atmosphere.

NONFERROUS METAL: Metals that are composed primarily of some element or elements other than iron.

OFFICER OF THE WATCH (OOW): Officer on duty in the engineering spaces.

OIL KING: A petty officer who receives, transfers, discharges, and tests fuel oil and maintains fuel oil records.

OIL POLLUTION ACTS: The Oil Pollution Act of 1924 (as amended) and the Oil Pollution Act of 1961 prohibit the overboard discharge of oil and water containing oil in port, in any sea area within 50 miles of land, and in special prohibited zones.

ORIFICE: A small opening.

OVERLOAD RELAY: An electrical protective device which automatically trips when a circuit draws excessive current.

OXIDATION: The process of various elements and compounds combining with oxygen. The corrosion of metals is generally a form of oxidation; rust on iron, for example, is iron oxide or oxidation.

PANT, PANTING: A series of pulsations caused by minor, recurrent explosions in the firebox of a ship's boiler. Usually caused by a shortage of air.

PERIPHERY: The curved line which forms the boundary of a circle (circumference), ellipse, or similar figure.

PITOMETER LOG: Device for indicating speed of ship and distance traveled by measuring water pressure on a tube projected outside the ship's hull.

PLASTICITY: That property which enables a material to be excessively and permanently deformed without breaking.

PNEUMERCATOR: A type of manometer used for measuring the volume of liquid in tanks.

PPM (PARTS PER MILLION): A comparison of the number of parts of a substance in a million parts of another substance. Used to measure the salt content of water.

PREHEATING: The application of heat to the base metal prior to a welding or cutting operation.

PRIME MOVER: The source of motion as a turbine, automobile engine, etc.

PUNCHING TUBES: The name applied to the mechanical means of cleaning the interiors of boiler tubes.

RADIATION, HEAT: The process of emitting heat in the form of heat waves.

REACH RODS: A length of pipe or back stock used as an extension on valve stems.

REACTION TURBINE: A turbine in which the major part of the driving force is received from the reactive force of steam leaving the blading.

REDUCER: Any coupling or fitting which connects a large opening to a smaller pipe or hose.

REDUCING VALVES: Automatic valves which are used to provide a steady pressure lower than the supply pressure.

REDUCTION GEAR: A set of gears used to transmit the rotation of one shaft to another at a slower speed.

REEFER: A provision cargo ship or a refrigerated compartment. An authorized abbreviation for refrigerator.

REFRIGERANT 12 (R-12): A nonpoisonous gas that is used in air conditioning and refrigeration systems.

REGULATOR (GAS): An instrument used to control the flow of gases from compressed gas cylinders.

REMOTE OPERATING GEAR: Flexible cables attached to valve wheels which permit the valves to be operated from another compartment.

RISER: A vertical pipe leading off a larger one; e.g., fireman riser.

ROOT VALVE: A valve located where a branch line comes off the main line.

ROTARY SWITCH: An electrical switch which closes or opens the circuit by a rotating motion.

SAE: Society of Automotive Engineers.

SAFETY VALVES: An automatic, quick opening and closing valve which has a reseat-pressure lower than the lift pressure.

SALINOMETER: A hydrometer that measures the concentration of salt in a solution.

SATURATION PRESSURE: The pressure corresponding to the saturation temperature.

SATURATION TEMPERATURE: The temperature at which a liquid boils under a given pressure. For any given saturation temperature there is a corresponding saturation pressure.

SCALE: Undesirable deposit, mostly calcium sulfate, which forms in the tubes of boilers.

SENTINEL VALVES: Small relief valves used primarily as a warning device.

SHAFT ALLEY: The long compartment of a ship in which the propeller shafts revolve.

SKETCH: A rough drawing indicating major features of an object to be constructed.

SLIDING FEET: A mounting for turbines and boilers to allow for expansion and contraction.

SLUDGE: The sediment left in fuel oil tanks.

SOLID COUPLING: A device used to join two shafts rigidly.

SOOT BLOWER: A soot removal device using a steam jet to clean the firesides of a boiler.

SPECIFIC HEAT: The amount of heat required to raise the temperature of one gram of a substance $1^{\circ}C$. All substances are compared to water which has a specific heat of 1.

SPEED-LIMITING GOVERNOR: A device for limiting the rotational speed of a prime mover.

SPEED-REGULATING GOVERNOR: A device that maintains a constant speed on a piece of machinery that is operating under varying load conditions.

SPLIT PLANT: A method of operating propulsion plants so that they are divided into two or more separate and complete units.

SPRING BEARINGS: Bearings positioned at various intervals along a propulsion shaft to help keep it in alignment and support its weight.

SPRINKLING SYSTEM: An automatic watering system used for cooling and flooding magazines and cargo spaces in case of fire.

STATIC: A force exerted by reason of weight alone, related to bodies at rest or in balance.

STEAM LANCE: A device for using low pressure steam inside of boilers to remove soot and carbon from boiler tubes.

STEERING ENGINE: The machinery that turns the rudder.

STERN TUBE: A watertight enclosure for the propeller shaft.

STRAIN: The deformation or change in shape of a material resulting from the applied load.

STRENGTH: The ability of a material to resist strain.

STRESS: Force producing or tending to produce deformation of a metal.

STUFFING BOX: A device to prevent leakage between a moving and a fixed part in a steam engineering plant.

STUFFING TUBE: A packed tube making a watertight fitting through a bulkhead for a cable or small pipe.

SUMP: A container, compartment, or reservoir; used as a drain or receptacle for fluids.

SUPERHEATER: A unit in the boiler that drys the steam and raises its temperature.

SWASH PLATES: Metal plates in the lower part of the steam drum that prevent the surging of boiler water with the motion of the ship.

SWITCHBOARD: A panel or group of panels with automatic protective devices, used to distribute the electrical power throughout the ship.

TANK TOP: Top side of tank section or double bottom of a ship.

TDC (TOP DEAD CENTER): The position of a reciprocating piston at its uppermost point of travel.

TEMPERING: The heating and controlled cooling of a metal to produce the desired hardness.

THIEF SAMPLE: A sample of oil or water taken from a ship's tank for analysis.

THROTTLEMAN: Man in the engineroom who operates the throttles to control the main engines.

THRUST BEARING: A bearing designed to limit the end play and absorb the axial thrust of a shaft.

TO BLOW TUBES: A procedure, using steam, for removing soot and carbon from the tubes of steaming boilers.

TOP OFF: To fill up, as a ship tops off in fuel oil before leaving port.

TOUGHNESS: That property of a material which enables it to withstand shock, and to be deformed without breaking.

TRANSFORMER: An electrical device used to step up or step down an a-c voltage.

TRICK WHEEL: A steering wheel in the steering engineroom or emergency steering station of a ship.

TUBE EXPANDER: A tool used to expand replacement tubes into their seats in boiler drums and headers.

TURBINE: A multibladed rotor, driven by steam or hot gas.

TURBINE JACKING GEAR: A motor-driven gear arrangement used to slowly rotate idle propulsion shafts and turbines.

TURBINE STAGE: The term applied to one set of nozzles and the succeeding row or rows of moving blades.

UPTAKES (EXHAUST TRUNKS): Large enclosed passages for exhaust gases from boilers to the stacks.

VENT: A valve in a tank or compartment used primarily to permit air to escape.

VENTURI INJECTOR: A device used for washing the firesides of boilers.

VOID: A small empty compartment below decks.

VOLATILE: The term used to describe a liquid that vaporizes quickly.

VOLTAGE TESTER (WIGGINS): A portable instrument that is used to detect electricity.

WATER TUBE BOILER: Boilers in which the water flows through the tubes and is heated by the gases of combustion.

WATER WASHING: A method of cleaning the firesides of boilers to remove soot and carbon.

WELDING LEAD: The conductor through which the electrical current is transmitted from the power source to the electrode holder and welding rod.

WHELPS: Any of the ribs or ridges on the barrel of a capstan or windlass.

WIREWAYS: Passageways, between decks and on the overheads of compartments, that contain electric cables.

WORK REQUEST: Request issued to a naval shipyard, tender, or repair ship for repairs.

ZERK FITTING: A small fitting to which a grease gun can be applied to force lubricating grease into bearings or moving parts of machinery.

ZINC: A metal placed in salt water systems to counteract the effects of electrolysis.

www.ingramcontent.com/pod-product-compliance
Lightning Source LLC
Chambersburg PA
CBHW080933020526
44116CB00033B/2524